ACCLAIM FOR
ACCESSIBLE GOSPEL, INCLUSIVE WORSHIP:

Accessible Gospel, Inclusive Worship is, without a doubt, Barbara Newman's finest work! Practicing what she preaches, Barbara has made this book so accessible to the reader: in its thoughtful tone, in its practical content, and in its logical structure. Not only is *Accessible Gospel, Inclusive Worship* incredibly well-designed, easy to understand, and hands-on in its applications — it is also solidly grounded biblically. Without reservation, I know I will enthusiastically recommend this book for years to come! I genuinely believe it is destined to become a classic work in the arena of disability and the Church.

—Stephanie O. Hubach
Director, Mission to North America Special Needs Ministries
Author of Same Lake, Different Boat: Coming Alongside People Touched by Disability

This accessible, practical, and profound book conveys an outpouring of love for God and for all of God's children. And it's contagious! People of all ages and with all kinds of complementary abilities and capacities who immerse themselves in the practices described in this book will find themselves growing in grace and knowledge of Jesus Christ. The depth of insight in this book arises from gratitude and wonder at the kind of frank communication depicted in the biblical Psalms. It's a vision that can strengthen both private prayer and public worship, and help us discover again the sheer joy of learning together in the body of Christ.

–John D. Witvliet
Director, Calvin Institute of Christian Worship
Professor, Calvin College and Calvin Theological Seminary

Barbara Newman is a master weaver. In this short and empowering book, she uses scripture and story as her loom, multisensory ways of understanding every person and communicating with them as the warp, and eight core actions of worship (The "Vertical Habits" from the Calvin Institute of Christian Worship) as the woof to create an imaginative and tested resource guide that can guide the whole church community in weaving everyone's gifts and needs into its life in worship and spiritual growth. Her simple but profound message: God included everyone, now it is up to us to be creative enough to practice what we preach.

–Bill Gaventa
M.Div., Director, Summer Institute on Theology and Disability

Barbara Newman just gets it! In her new book, *Accessible Gospel, Inclusive Worship*, Barbara gives us practical hands-on strategies and hope-filled stories helping all of us see that inclusion is more than just possible...it's essential.

–Emily Colson
Author of *Dancing with Max*

Barbara Newman's new book, *Accessible Gospel, Inclusive Worship* provides church leaders and family members with a very practical model for not just helping kids with disabilities to come to know Christ, but to help each child grow in their faith. This book needs to be in the hands of everyone serving in children's, youth, family or disability ministry, and every parent or grandparent seeking to promote the spiritual growth of the children in their life impacted by disability.

–Stephen Grcevich
MD, Founder/Director of Strategic Initiatives
Key Ministry

Newman weaves practical advice with poignant stories that illustrate both loving inclusion and painful exclusion of children and youth with disabilities in church life. Anyone involved in church education with involves children or youth will find *Accessible Gospel, Inclusive Worship* an excellent resource.

–Rev. Mark Stephenson
Director, Disability Concerns
Christian Reformed Church in North America

As always, this is wonderfully practical Barbara Newman work. *Accessible Gospel, Inclusive Worship* is a guide to belonging and relationship in the expression of faith, whether pastor, parent or practitioner. Barbara draws me in as a reader in the same compelling way as all are invited together in worship. Through fresh perspectives, personal stories, and innovative ideas of senses and movement, we are reminded that the Gospel in our midst is surely the most inclusive thing of all.

–David Morstad
Executive Director
Bethesda Institute

This is good news for churches seeking to live as God's covenant people and desiring to make a lasting impact on all who God entrusts to them.

–Terry A. DeYoung
Coordinator, Disability Concerns
Reformed Church in America

Accessible Gospel, Inclusive Worship

Accessible Gospel, Inclusive Worship

by Barbara J. Newman
with contributions by Betty Grit

Published by CLC Network

CLC Network
Christian Learning Center

clcnetwork.org

Also by Barbara J. Newman:

Nuts and Bolts of Inclusive Education. CLC Network, 2013.

El Autismo Y Tu Iglesia Faith Alive Christian Resources/ Libros Desafio, 2013 (Spanish Translation of Autism and Your Church, 2012).

Autism: A Christian Response DVD. CLC Network, 2012.

The Behavior Management Playing Field DVD. CLC Network, 2012.

Helping Kids Include Kids with Disabilities. Faith Alive Christian Resources, 2012 (Revised from 2001).

Including Children with Disabilities: Preparing a Place of Welcome DVD. CLC Network, 2012.

Inclusion Tool Box: 52 Ideas to Include Individuals with Disabilities DVD. CLC Network, 2012.

Making Room: Cultivating Communities of Inclusion – G.L.U.E. Manual and DVD. (with Kimberly Luurtsema, Dr. Andrew J. Bandstra, Dr. Thomas B. Hoeksema, Ralph and Carol Honderd) CLC Network, 2012.

Autism and Your Church – Nurturing the Spiritual Growth of People with Autism Spectrum Disorders. Faith Alive Christian Resources, 2011 (Revised from 2006).

Body Building: Devotions to Celebrate Inclusive Community. CLC Network, 2011 (Revised from 2009).

Any Questions? A Guidebook for Inclusive Education. CLC Network, 2009.

Church Welcome Story. CLC Network, 2009.

Circle of Friends Manual. CLC Network, 2009.

G.L.U.E. Training Manual: Working Closely with Congregations to Help Them Better Understand, Support and Include Each Other. (with Kimberly Luurtsema) CLC Network, 2009.

School Welcome Story. CLC Network, 2009.

Special Needs Smart Pages created by Joni and Friends. (Contributing writer) Gospel Light, 2009.

Inclusion Awareness Kit. CLC Network, 2008.

Easter Book: A Resource for Leaders and Mentors. Faith Alive Christian Resources, 2003.

This book is dedicated to our husbands, Barry Newman and Nelson Grit. During the preparation of this book, the Newmans celebrated 25 years of marriage and the Grits celebrated 50 years of marriage. We are so thankful for the support and love of our husbands over so many years together. Best friends and partners in ministry – we praise God for you.

Library of Congress Cataloging-in-Publication Data

Newman, Barbara J., 1962-

Accessible Gospel, Inclusive Worship

ISBN 978-1-936100-14-9

clcnetwork.org

4340 Burlingame Avenue SW | Wyoming, MI 49509
p: (616) 245.8388 | f: (616) 243.3662
e: info@clcnetwork.org

ACKNOWLEDGEMENT

This book was made possible by a couple who treasures the working triangle of a Christian family with a Christian school and with a solid, evangelical church. We treasure God's gift of children with whatever abilities and needs they may have and believe that all children are covenant children and should be taught and treated with respect, love, and care.

With thanks to Dr. John Witvliet of the Calvin Institute of Christian Worship, Bruce Gritter, and Karen Wilk for developing the framework of Vertical Habits and to the many congregations and schools who have taught and practiced the concept and shared their reflections and resources with us.

With thanks to the following individuals who have contributed specific Vertical Habits projects and images to this book: Bruce Benedict, Randy Beumer, Matt Hale, Kris Moore, Kyle Ragsdale, Dawn Rotman, Jeffrey Sajdak, Mona Roozeboom and Judie Zwiers.

With thanks to Dr. Andrew Bandstra, Victoria White, and the team at CLC Network for their work in editing this book.

TABLE OF CONTENTS

Here I Stand by Kyle Ragsdale

INTRODUCTION

CONFERENCE STORY AND THE IMPORTANCE
OF THIS MATERIAL

I'll never forget the look on her face. I was attending a conference many years ago; the speaker was a well-known and brilliant individual with autism spectrum disorder (ASD). There was a time slot where people could ask some questions. Across the crowded room, a woman expectantly raised her hand. The speaker acknowledged her. "I have a daughter with autism. Do you have any advice on how we can introduce my daughter to God?" Without hesitating and with finality in her words, the speaker said, "God is too hard for people with autism to understand. Next question." My eyes went immediately to this mom. Her face dropped, her coloring changed, and then the tears started to flow. I could see the devastation from many rows away. When the session was over, I tried to push my way past people to get to this mom – to reassure her that I have several friends with ASD who have a vibrant relationship with Jesus Christ. When I got to her seating section, she was gone. I looked for her in the women's restroom, in the eating area, and in the remaining sessions to no avail.

This day of training many years ago and the face of this mother is permanently etched on my brain. In fact, it's her face I see in every writing session for this book. On that day, I was unable to reach her.

Maybe you have been asking that question too. I hear it a lot from parents and leaders within church communities. How do I know my child with a disability is saved? How do I introduce my friend with a disability to Jesus Christ? How can my adult child grow in the faith? While I have the opportunity to speak on many topics across the country, the topic of accessible gospel and inclusive worship is the most treasured to me. It's the reason for every other topic on my speaking list. Behavior management is important because it creates an environment where you best have the attention of those participating. Creating inclusive churches is important because, in addition to home, they often provide the setting where spiritual formation happens over an individual's lifetime. Autism spectrum disorder, sensory processing disorder, understanding persons with an intellectual disability or AD/HD are also important topics because the information allows us to better select tools when interacting with a person with a specific disability area. Creating understanding and welcoming peers is another speaking topic because inclusive community provides places for everyone to grow one step closer to Jesus Christ – and each person is critical in that process to one another. And while I often travel with a suitcase filled with aprons that display pictures, recordable buttons that offer options for persons with no spoken words, gadgets for those who struggle with writing or reading, and seating options for those with attention concerns, these tools all feed the process of meeting Jesus and growing in Him.

If I had reached the mom on that day of the conference, I would have spoken with her about the process and methods I describe in this book. In lieu of that conversation, I offer this to you. May you experience God's presence and clear direction as you walk through this material. Whether you are currently mom, dad, grandma, grandpa, sibling, Church school teacher, adult group leader, mentor, classroom assistant, pastor, or friend to the individual that brought you to this book, may you also enjoy relating as a brother or sister in Jesus Christ.

THOUGHTS ABOUT SPIRITUAL FORMATION

My dear children, for whom I am again in the pains of childbirth until Christ is formed in you. Galatians 4:19

I am not a theologian; I am a special education teacher. While I am a devoted follower of Jesus Christ, this book is about practical ideas, not theological understanding. And yet, as is true for most Christian authors, one must have a working knowledge of the topic from a biblical base before launching into ideas to try. Theologians such as Dallas Willard[1] and N.T. Wright[2] have produced some excellent books and articles on the topic of **spiritual formation** and growing in the disciplines of the faith. Some people might use the words **faith formation** to describe this process as well. In my quest for more information, I not only did some reading, but I also interviewed some pastors and theologians for a starting place in thinking about this topic before relating it specifically to persons with disabilities.

Pastor Rich Hamstra from First Christian Reformed Church in Grand Haven, Michigan offered three phrases that he believes capture the heart of spiritual formation.

"Meaningfully devoted" "Use of gifts in service" "Presentation of one's witness"

To further add to these thoughts, Pastor Randy Bremmer from Trinity Reformed Church in Grand Haven, Michigan stated, "I prefer 'Christian formation' because 'spiritual formation' is too vague and could mean just about anything. It's the process of recreating a unique representation of Christ in the life of the believer."

It has been a huge joy in my life to be the daughter of a theologian. So, as with many questions, I decided to ask my dad. He is also professor emeritus of New Testament and Theology at Calvin Theological Seminary in Grand Rapids, Michigan. As he reviewed the comments from Pastors Hamstra and Bremmer, Dr. Andrew J. Bandstra added, "I agree; however, we must emphasize the role of the Holy Spirit in the process as well."

Dr. John Witvliet of the Calvin Institute of Christian Worship affirmed that direction with his comments. "Christian formation is the way the Holy Spirit shapes and molds us to become disciples of Jesus. We are privileged to participate in the Spirit's work by 'walking in step with the Spirit,' praying in the Spirit, reading the Spirit-inspired Scripture, and obeying the gracious Spirit-inspired commands found in Scripture—including commands to worship God, hear the Word preached, celebrate the sacraments, pray together, share the good news, and express hospitality."

Still on a search for a working definition, I noted that Zeeland Christian School (ZCS) offers a statement on their website. I have had a classroom at ZCS for the past 26 years, and I believe they offer a direction that weaves in the comments of those I read and those I interviewed. "We create an environment where students, through the work of the Holy Spirit, are encouraged to develop a personal faith in Jesus Christ so that God can use them to impact His world."[3]

Using these thoughts, ideas, and readings as background, I hope to address the following question in this book: **How can we set up an environment where persons with disabilities can connect with the gospel message and grow in relationship with Jesus Christ?**

I find this question freeing and delightful. In fact, it's important to "let ourselves off the hook" in some ways. Salvation is a gift from God. *For it is by grace you have been saved, through faith – and this not from yourselves, it is the gift of God.* Ephesians 2:8. You and I are not the ones who save; that is God's work and His gift. I do believe, however, we are called to set up environments where we can make an introduction between the Lord of our lives and those we love and know. Those environments may take some creativity we have not yet imagined. How do we construct these places of introduction for persons with an intellectual disability, autism spectrum disorder, or other areas of disability?

It is also important, I believe, to offer environments where each one is able to grow in relationship with Jesus Christ. While the church we attend may be "handicap accessible," how much energy and effort do we invest in making our worship services accessible? It's not just about being able to get inside the church physically, it's also about being able to have each one enter into that conversation with God. As we engage in prayer, praise, listening, learning, confessing, serving, and blessing, whether with family at home or our family at church, it's an opportunity to grow in our relationship with Jesus Christ. How do we create those kinds of accessible conversations and activities for each one?

If you are hungry for some very practical ideas in setting up those environments and introductions, may this book be a valuable resource for you to use.

How Can I Help by Randy Beumer

PLANTING OUR FEET ON COMMON GROUND: THE PUZZLE PIECE PERSPECTIVE

PUZZLE PIECES

For many years I have been intrigued with the idea of green and pink puzzle pieces. My car, suitcase, or desk generally has at least one of them close by. The puzzle piece is half green and half pink. Doug Bouman, School Psychologist at CLC Network, introduced me to those colors many years ago. As we look more deeply into the talents and areas of concern in children and adults, it's clear that we are each a combination of greens and pinks. Green represents our areas of gifting and strength. Like the trees, grass, and growth in creation, we each have green spots. Pink, however, is also part of each life. It represents the "hot spots" and areas of weakness or concern. While perhaps not our favorite parts, we each have pink spots too. Psalm 139:13 says, *For you created my inmost being; you knit me together in my mother's womb.* I suspect that as God knit each one of us, He used green and pink yarn.

As I reflect on my own life, it's clear to see both the green and pink parts. Green for me is anything having to do with words. I love words. I enjoy reading them, writing them, and speaking them – although my husband is quick to point out that sometimes this green can become a pink if I speak too many words! I have a Facebook account primarily to play word games with my friends and family. Scrabble, Boggle, Quiddler, and Words with Friends are all at the top of my list of favorites. Pink for me, however, is anything having to do with eye-hand coordination. When my sons ask me to play one of their video games, it's generally because they will win and I will lose. If you throw a ball at me, don't expect me to catch it, kick it, or strike it. That's very difficult for me.

What about you? What are your green areas of strength and your pink areas of struggle? Is your puzzle piece similar to mine or is it the exact opposite? Would you rather play on your church softball team or offer the prayer in front of a group of people? For the sake of this topic, think for a few minutes about your gift areas. What is easy for you? Some people may pick speaking or writing, while others may excel in making a pie, taking apart and reassembling a car engine, showing hospitality, or singing. What is it for you?

What is green for you?

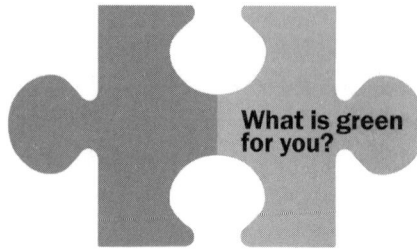

Likewise, what are your pink spots? Perhaps you joined me in grade 4 – last one against the wall to be picked for the recess sport team. Perhaps it's difficult for you to pay attention, keep things organized, spell, use numbers, or bake. What is pink for you?

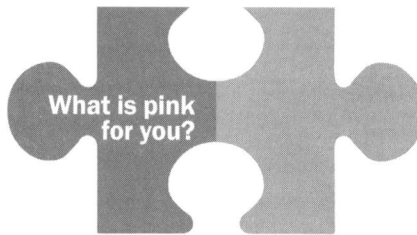

What is pink for you?

LESSONS LEARNED FROM PUZZLE PIECES

As you examine your own puzzle piece, consider some of the lessons they can teach us. First, God does not make puzzle pieces that are all pink. Scripture is clear. Each one has been given a gift to bring to the body of believers – a gift that can encourage and build that community. *Instead, speaking the truth in love, we will grow to become in every respect the mature body of Him who is the head, that is, Christ. From Him the whole body, joined and held together by every supporting ligament, grows and builds itself up in love, as each part does its work.* Ephesians 4:15-16

While we know this is true, how often do we hear people assume that a person with a disability is an "all pink" person? "This is Down syndrome Clayton." "Meet Cerebral Palsy Sue." "You must be Autistic Simone." "This is wheelchair Carlos." It's as though the person's disability completely defines that individual's life. As Christians, however, it's clear to see that this is not "Down syndrome Clayton." Rather, this is Clayton. He has been hand-knit and designed by God to fill a specific spot in His kingdom. God has given him gifts to use within the body of Christ, and he is to be considered an honored and indispensable member of that body. Clayton is a dearly loved child of God who also happens to have Down syndrome as part of his God-given design. While those outside our Christian communities may have a different pair of eyeglasses when viewing Clayton, our lenses have been crafted by God – and our vision is clear about Clayton's worth and importance.

Another lesson from our puzzle pieces suggests that God did not make any pieces that are all green. There is no one who gets an all green life; we are combinations of strengths and weaknesses. While I would have gladly traded mine in for an "all green" puzzle piece as I was waiting against the recess wall to be chosen for some team, that was also not God's design. While there are undoubtedly many reasons for God's design pattern, I suspect one of the reasons God makes us a combination of strengths and struggles is that He designed us to need one another. If I were all green, I would not need any of you. In a church setting, I could preach the sermon, design the banners on the walls, create the written publications, run the nursery, make tasty meals for those recently home from the hospital, serve as a greeter, do the landscaping, and fix the air conditioning when it breaks. Whether in a church, family, school, or community setting, we need to tap into the gifts of each one in order to function best. I was designed to need others.

Another lesson of these puzzle pieces is that they link together. Places where I am strong, I can come alongside of you. Places where you are strong, you can support me. We fit together like a puzzle in the body of Christ. Not only did God hand-craft each individual, He also takes time to arrange them into communities. 1 Corinthians 12:18 says, *But in fact God has placed the parts in the body, every one of them, just as He wanted them to be.* Your presence in a community or family is no mistake. You have been beautifully designed and then PLACED by your creator.

THE PUZZLE PIECE PERSPECTIVE

When we put on the puzzle piece lenses, it impacts our actions, attitudes, and word choices. Imagine God hand-designing an individual and placing that person in the middle of a congregation. Yet, when the family visits the church, a leader approaches them and says, "Sorry. We don't really have anything for you here." Imagine a puzzle piece being sent away – one that God had intended to use to make that congregation stronger. In this case, who loses? I would contend everyone loses. The individual does not have access to the richness of the church setting and the congregation loses out on the gift God had intended to place with them.

The puzzle piece perspective impacts the words we use when visiting a mom and dad in the hospital who just gave birth to a child with Spina Bifida. It allows us to focus on the child. We can comment on the child's hair color, his eyes looking just like mom's eyes, the length of labor and delivery, and what color they painted the nursery. You might also ask about issues related to Spina Bifida, but the focus is on the fact that a child was born – not a disability. How about the announcement in church the next Sunday? Should it sound like a funeral announcement? "I regret to inform you that Maggie and Jeff just gave birth to..." To what? A disability or a child? The puzzle piece perspective reminds us that a child has been born and we as a congregation will have a chance to grow and learn because of the child's presence.

What about the family who has a child with autism spectrum disorder signed up for Church school? Some ignore the puzzle piece perspective. They approach the parent and say, "I see Justin is signed up for Church school. What's wrong with him?" This focuses on the pink part first. The whole world does this. Justin's parents have been in countless meetings where they discuss how many degrees below zero, how dysfunctional, how atypical, and how deficient Justin is. We don't need to do this! Be a welcome breath of fresh air. Armed with your puzzle piece spectacles, talk with the parent and say, "I see Justin is signed up for Church school. We are so glad to have him be part of this group. What does he love to do?" What a different conversation you can have!

Puzzle pieces could make a difference in what we name our opportunities in churches and other settings. Do you really want to minister TO a person with a disability? Are we offering a ministry FOR that person? While there are times each of us need to be ministered to, those prepositions would seem to indicate that you are the green one and she is the pink one. Would you rather minister WITH a person with a disability? Could we help facilitate friendships instead of leaders and followers? If you spend any time at all with persons with disabilities, you will know that you have learned, received, and benefited from the relationship. So, let's be honest with our names. Places where I am strong, I can help someone else. Places where I am weak, that individual can help me. Lets make sure our written information and group names reflect that philosophy.

The puzzle piece perspective also helps us as we think about how to create an environment for presenting an accessible gospel message. It wouldn't make much sense to craft a "one size fits all" set of materials for presenting the gospel. Each individual is a unique blend of greens and pinks. We would first want to get to know that individual well; we will want to study God's knitting pattern in that person. From that base, it will be much easier to select an idea that fits our friend, child, or student.

In the same fashion, designing opportunities for inclusive worship will also be individualized and based on the unique gifts and needs of that person. A worship experience for someone who uses pictures to communicate will present different options than for a person who uses spoken words. We need to become experts on Tom and McKayla as we find ways to worship together.

Finally, the puzzle pieces offer a kind of promise to those committed to this process. Finding places where all can worship together will clearly benefit the entire body of Christ as we link our puzzle piece lives together. 1 Corinthians 12 is loaded with information to remind us that each part of the body is critical.

The eye cannot say to the hand, "I don't need you!" And the head cannot say to the feet, "I don't need you!" On the contrary, those parts of the body that seem to be weaker are indispensable, and the parts that we think are less honorable we treat with special honor. And the parts that are unpresentable are treated with special modesty, while our presentable parts need no special treatment. But God has put the body together, giving greater honor to the parts that lacked it, so that there should be no division in the body, but that its parts should have equal concern for each other. If one part suffers, every part suffers with it; if one part is honored, every part rejoices with it. Now you are the body of Christ, and each one of you is a part of it. 1 Corinthians 12:21-27

Pastor Mark Stephenson is quick to point out that we must be very cautious in making assumptions about which body parts are the "weak ones."[1] While we may bring a certain perspective, this Scripture passage points out God may not share our perspective. "Those parts that seem to be weaker" suggests that it is our assumption, not God's assumption.

Designing environments for worship where we can each tell God "I love you" and we can each say the prayer words "Help me" will undoubtedly add a richness not yet imagined by some congregations. As I watch a prayer uttered with sign language or movements, my own verbal prayer can take on new meaning.

Sitting close by us in church is a young adult named Brendan. Brendan's puzzle piece is delightful. Green for Brendan is rhythm and music. He brings joy through his expressive smile, and he is an expert on Mario and Luigi. Pink for him is clearly spoken words and some areas of academic learning. Brendan loves church, but especially music – any music. In a church that can sometimes take jabs at one another musically – some preferring the hymnbook and others preferring songs heard on popular contemporary Christian radio programs – Brendan is our model. His enthusiasm, joy, and movements are equally applied to Charles Wesley's hymn "Oh for a thousand tongues to sing" and Matt Redman's contemporary song "Ten thousand reasons for my heart to find." Wesley and Redman ignite a connection with God in Brendan in a way that is infectious to those around him. He has brought a sort of glue to our worship experiences.

Would you like additional ways to use these puzzle pieces within a group at your church, school, or family?

Think about the *Inclusion Awareness Kit*[2] as a way to bring this concept to your community. It's available at www.clcnetwork.org.

Help! by Kyle Ragsdale

MOST IMPORTANT PLACE TO BEGIN: GETTING TO KNOW THE INDIVIDUAL

INTRODUCTION

I want to introduce you to a process. Although it's a standard process that can be used with many people, the outcomes are individualized based on that person's unique God-given strengths and struggles. To help make this as practical as possible, there is a form in Appendix A you can use in working through the next several pages of this book. Please turn to Appendix A and follow the instructions on where to find a printable version of these pages. If you use that form along with the written suggestions, you will be well on your way to discovering some strategies to try.

PLACE TO BEGIN: PUZZLE PIECES

On page 86 you will see a green and pink puzzle piece. If you have a specific person that brought you to this book, fill in the puzzle piece for that person. What gifts, interests, and talents can you list on the green side for this person? What about difficult areas and weaknesses? List those on the pink side. Try to come up with 3-5 greens and 2-3 pinks. When you have written them down, thank God for the areas of gifting you see in this individual.

ASKING THE RIGHT QUESTION: WHAT CAN THE INDIVIDUAL DO?

As we continue to get to know this individual, it's important to ask the right questions. So often we focus on what that person CAN'T do. She can't sing, he can't speak, she can't write, he can't walk. While these things may be true, they rarely lead us to any strategies to try. It seems important to ask the right question – What CAN the person do? She can wave a praise streamer, he can point to a picture to communicate, she can use a computer that converts her speech to written words, and he can steer his wheelchair (in fact, he pops wheelies in the hallway!). When you focus on what a person is able to do and what that individual enjoys, it's much easier to think of the tools, approach, and opportunities to include in that environment where we can make this most important introduction.

HOW DOES THE INDIVIDUAL TAKE INFORMATION IN?

If we think about a typical classroom or church service, those in charge often assume that most people take in information through spoken words. Instructions and information are often given typically orally. So often "word learners" are drawn to positions such as pastors or teachers. Presenters assume that others take information in the same way. That group of ear learners, however, is dwindling. How often do people comment that they learned and remembered so much from the children's message because they were shown an object or picture? It's important to know how people best process information so that we can align our strategies with that person's best way of taking information in.

Some people do function well with words. Others prefer pictures or objects. Adding a photo or branch of an oak tree can make a sermon illustration come alive. Other individuals may understand best with a sign language interpreter or materials available in Braille or large print. Some people take information in through reading. The level of a person's reading ability may be important to know as you continue this process.

Two other factors greatly impact the area of information processing. First, how well does this person remember? What tools help this person retain information? As we think of presenting information to an individual, we also want to increase the chance of a person remembering the information. Adding rhythm and movement can often greatly improve the chance of a person remembering a Bible verse. Keeping a visual on the wall of main concepts can assist long-term memory. Boiling down information to one main point and repeating that point verbally, visually, and with movements can also help retention.

In general, the greater number of sensory systems you involve, the higher likelihood a person will remember. God set a perfect example for us. In the Bible He set up a way to "remember me" in Communion. He involved five sensory systems in the process, increasing the likelihood we will all remember. Partaking of the Lord's Supper is something we can see, touch, taste, and smell. When combined with God's instructions in Scripture, we can also hear it. God set the gold standard for us to follow in remembering!

The second factor that can greatly impact information processing is the ability to pay attention. You can have the most amazing set of materials combined with a dramatic flair you could take to Hollywood, but if the person has an attention span of two minutes, that's the time you have to input information before capturing another two-minute time block sometime in the future. The good news is that there are some good supports to use to help lengthen and strengthen a person's attention. For example, instead of only offering chairs to sit in, some people can pay attention for a longer time by sitting on something with air in it such as an exercise ball or inflatable seat cushion. Some companies are even making desk tops that are attached to exercise bikes and treadmills. Some people enjoy holding something to fidget with while trying to listen and focus. Allowing people choices to move can also be helpful. Standing and listening can be far more effective for some people than sitting and listening. Another strategy to help someone focus is to break the day or the task into smaller parts. Having a schedule with words or pictures that people can move or check off when finished can be a great way to hold someone's attention. This works especially well when the last item on the schedule is something the individual really enjoys. From seat cushions to visual schedules, attention span is a critical part of taking information in.

Using the form from Appendix A, jot some notes about the individual that brought you to this book. How does this person take information in? You can also make note of questions you might want to ask so that you can get this kind of information.

HOW DOES THE INDIVIDUAL GET INFORMATION OUT?

We communicate in a wide variety of ways. Without any words at all, a new-born has excellent communication skills. You can tell if the child is peaceful, upset, tired, content, or fussy just by the way the baby holds his body or cries. He can command an entire set of adults with just a few communication tools. If you think about your day today, you can probably make a long list of ways you communicated to others. It might have been with body language, a gesture, spoken words, pointing to something, or writing a note. As we get to know an individual even more closely, it's important to understand some of the communication tools this person can use. Can the individual speak words and how much meaning do those spoken words have? For example, some people repeat phrases, but the actual words may have little meaning to the individual. Some people will take your arm or hand and pull you to a desired object. Another person might get information out by writing. Again, it's important to know how much a person can write and what kind of meaning those words have. Some individuals have learned to copy words while others use that as a prime way to tell you what they need or want. In addition, some people need specific types of pencils or grips in order to write legibly. Make sure you have some available in your environment. Some individuals use sign language or gestures to communicate. Others may draw pictures or symbols.

If an individual is without spoken words, many speech therapists will recommend using pictures to communicate. You could take a picture of the three snacks you are offering that day, and the individual points to the picture of the snack that looks the best. Some people string pictures and symbols together to form sentences. A person might display the phrase "I want crackers please" through a series of 3-4 pictures. If a person uses pictures to communicate, it's important to have the tools available in your environment. Would you leave your voice at home? Then don't forget to pack the pictures either.

Technology has ushered in a whole new era of communication tools. If you own a smart phone, there's a good chance there is a setting that allows it to speak to you as well as turn your voice into written text. For a small monthly fee, you can get your voicemails turned into written words.[1] These kinds of tools are so helpful for persons who communicate without spoken words. There are so many different kinds of communication devices that give a spoken voice to the needs and wants of the person pushing the buttons or programming the device.

Make sure you understand how to listen to the individual you are with. Find out how that person communicates and what ways you can enter into that conversation together. Make sure they have access to the equipment needed to have a conversation together.

Take out the form from Appendix A. Jot down some notes in this section. You may also have a couple of questions you would like answered as you continue to get to know this individual. How does this person get information out?

WHAT MOVEMENTS CAN THE PERSON DO?

When I first met Marie at church, I wanted to say good morning and shake her hand. Marie uses a wheelchair and was pushed by a caregiver to the front row of the sanctuary. When I reached out to say good morning, I noted her wrists were in soft Velcro ties. As I started to speak, I noticed she was frantically moving her eyes up and down. Only a soft groan came out of her mouth. I smiled and walked away realizing that I needed to get the answer to this question: What movements can Marie do?

After speaking with her caregivers, I found out that she has voluntary control of her eyes only. When she looks at you, the answer is "yes." When she looks away, the answer is "no." She also has a board with a set of words and phrases on it. She keeps this in a bag on the back of her wheelchair. If you point to the columns, she will look at you to get your finger to stop moving. When you point to the rows, she will look at you again. The intersection of the row and column is the word or phrase she wants to say.

In order to interact with Marie in a meaningful way, I needed to understand her movements and what she could do. This could be helpful when interacting with your friend as well. Can he walk and run? Can she operate her own wheelchair? Can he sit in a chair on his own? Can she hold a spoon while eating? While your friend may have many movements that work well, for those individuals who have limited mobility, find out what tools, equipment, and safety issues impact the individual's ability to interact with the environment.

One word of caution. Make sure you separate physical differences and intellectual differences. So many people assume that my friend Marie has a lower IQ. This is not true. While her body has limited mobility, her ability to think, solve problems, and understand the world is very typical. She enjoys a great joke, a handsome man, and reads words easily.

On your form from Appendix A, what comments can you write about the individual in your life? What movements can this person do?

DOES THE INDIVIDUAL HAVE ANY SENSORY SENSITIVITIES?

I was visiting a friend. She has been diagnosed with Lyme Disease. This has greatly impacted her neurological system. We used to meet for a cup of coffee and a chat at Panera Bread; now it's much easier to meet at her home. She gets dizzy now and has become sensitive to the light. She wears sunglasses to protect her eyes and walks very slowly so she doesn't fall. Her home is usually quite dark inside, and those who visit use quieter voices because sounds can be overwhelming. The part of her brain that processes sensations like sounds, sights, tastes, balance, pain, touch, and smells has changed so much in the last couple of years. A trip to Panera Bread for a cup of coffee was one of many things she used to do in a day. Now it would be her only outing, require a driver to get there, and probably have her resting for the remainder of the day due to exhaustion. The coffee shop is filled with sensations that would be difficult for her brain to filter. My friend acquired these sensory sensitivities to sounds, sights, and movements due to Lyme Disease. They are hopeful these differences will fade with treatment. For other individuals, sensory differences last a lifetime. Many times, when there is a neurological difference, there is also a sensory difference. People are not making it up. The sounds you hear that seem typical could be painfully loud to another person. The volume understanding is in our brain – and it varies from individual to individual.

While I would encourage you to get more information on this topic, I will offer a brief explanation of sensory differences so you can better interact with your friend. Imagine sitting by a piano keyboard. Middle C is right in the center of that keyboard, and it's a great place to be for your senses. If your sensory system is wired at middle C, you can take in the sensations that are important, and you can block out the others. If you are sitting down and reading this book, you most likely are not focused on the way your rear end feels in the chair (at least not until I mentioned it). Your sensory system has blocked that out as unimportant information. If, however, you sit for too long and your body needs some blood moving around, your sensory system will send some input that has you shifting and moving so your body parts get the needed blood supply.

Some individuals have sensory systems that are set far above middle C in one or more areas. It may take a small amount of the sensation, and it registers in a big way. A small noise might have that person covering her ears because it sounds loud to her. Someone brushing past her in the church hallway might have her grabbing her arm and wondering who hit her. The perfume of the individual three rows away might have her gagging and leaving the sanctuary. Please remember, this is not a made-up situation. Her brain interprets those signals and the feeling is very real. As you can imagine, just as with my friend with Lyme Disease, settings with a lot of stimulation can pose large threats. If you are sensitive to noise, for example, a loud children's setting, a rambunctious youth group, and a worship team wired for big sound can all be challenging. While there are tools to help filter some of the sounds, please understand that persons venturing out into these environments deserve an award at the end of the day for bravery!

While there are people wired above middle C, you can also have individuals wired way below middle C. In this situation, a person would take a lot of input to even register the sensation. I had a student who slammed her fingers in a car door, looked at me calmly and said "ow." She had no tears or concern because her pain receptors are set up differently. She truly feels less pain, although the bruising on her fingers showed the extent of the injury. This difference can happen in any sensory system. A person could seem nearly oblivious to someone calling his or her name. You need great volume to register the sound. Another person might come up and squeeze you very tightly. He loves hard and heavy touch because he needs it that way for his brain to even know someone is there. In fact, if hard and heavy touch feels good to him, he could assume it also feels good to you. Most individuals believe other people's sensory systems are wired similarly. This is the cause of much misunderstanding and a really important lesson to teach! This under-sensitivity to sensations can happen in any sensory system.

While the cause for sensory differences varies, and the length of time one has this difference can vary, it's important to be aware of any unique wiring in the individual in your life. Remember, some individuals can have several differences. She might be under-sensitive in one area and over-sensitive in another. Using the form from Appendix A, consider some of the following information. While this is an overgeneralization and I am avoiding technical terms, here is what you might see:

Below Middle C Under-sensitive	Sensory System	Above Middle C Over-sensitive
Speaks loudly, needs a lot of sound to register, often doesn't hear spoken directions	Sound	Covers ears, avoids situations where there are unpredictable noises such as buzzers in a sporting event
Hard to register non-verbal cues such as body language, needs a lot of visual input before seeing something	Sight	Avoids eye contact, prefers environments where there are fewer decorations and visuals
Likes food spicy, bubbly, and hot; would be a great candidate for eating foods high on the Scofield Index	Taste	Has a limited number of foods that are safe, often eats more bland foods with a smooth texture
Seems oblivious to smells like rotten foods, dirty diapers, or body odor	Smell	Reacts strongly to smells such as perfume, hair gel, coffee breath, and detergents; might leave a room gagging
Craves touch, gives hard and strong hugs, likes to play rough and hard	Touch	Cuts tags from clothing, aligns sock on foot exactly, interprets light touch as pain, avoids getting touched unexpectedly
Likes to spin, hang upside down, and can ride roller coasters over and over with great joy	Balance	Avoids moving quickly, hugs the walls for support, looks down in crowded places
Moves around a lot on a chair to gather position, challenging to feel a pencil in hand	Muscle Feedback	Holds objects lightly, tries to limit some movements

Please note on the form from Appendix A what sensory differences you may see in the individual that brought you to this book. Perhaps you can find out what tools have been helpful for this individual to regulate that particular sensation. Tools like sound blockers, weighted vests, a brushing technique, tinted glasses, a mechanical pencil, a mini trampoline, and much more can make the difference between attending or not attending an event.

On your form from Appendix A, list the sensory differences for your individual.

WHAT EQUIPMENT, SAFETY MEASURES, OR SUPPORTS MIGHT BE IMPORTANT FOR THIS PERSON?

If you are the child's parent, you are the child's expert. If you are the adult's caregiver, you may also be an expert. It is really important in this category, however, to resource the other people who will be spending time with the child or adult. If you are not the individual's "expert," what information might you need to know? Do whatever you can to get this information.

We have children at our school who have seizures. We type up a safety protocol and have emergency supplies for each one. All the people who are part of the child's life know what to do if a seizure happens. We have children who have allergies to bee stings or certain foods. Each of these children has a safety protocol typed up and has emergency supplies available as needed. Each adult needs to know the process to follow and have access to the needed supplies. If you are interacting with an individual who has any medical issues that require emergency intervention, make sure you have a written plan in place.

For my friend Marie, the individual who speaks with her eyes, we needed to understand a lot about daily care in order to better include her. In order to take communion, you need to get a piece of bread very mushy with the juice and place it on the back of her tongue. Positioning her wheelchair is important to the aches and pains she feels every day. We needed to understand this. This category is long for Marie, and several people at church needed to be fully trained in how to come alongside her.

For the youth group member with AD/HD, you might need some equipment that is helpful for focusing. Having an exercise ball to sit on and a fidget pencil for writing could make a big difference in participation. For a struggling writer, having the right pencil, paper, and slant board could open doors for participation.

While it's not possible to cover all of the technology, equipment, or safety measures you may need to discover, remember that you are finding out about one person. What does Chaniqua need? What does Barry need? Become an expert on that one person and find out how to best equip your environment for safety and success.

On your form from Appendix A, list what you know and what you need to know.

WHO NEEDS TO KNOW THIS INFORMATION?

Every good plan has two parts. The first part of the plan involves the individual, while the second part of the plan involves "the others" who are part of the environment. Peers, volunteers, family members, pastors, work colleagues, and people at the community center might need to know pieces and parts of this plan. As we are creating this environment for access to the Gospel and inclusive worship, there will undoubtedly be others who are part of this arrangement.

For example, let's imagine that we are going to give Yolanda a streamer to wave during praise and worship time. This is a way she can say "I love you" to God without using words. If Yolanda begins to wave the streamer without informing the rest of the congregation, some might view her as a distraction.

It's important to think about equipping the rest of the congregation to better receive her gift of praise and worship. In one church I visited, the pastor simply said, "I've asked Yolanda to wave a purple streamer as we sing today. I am beginning a sermon series on Jesus as our king, and I want us to think about that as we worship." Is Yolanda a distraction now or is she part of the worship plan and team? By asking the question "Who needs to know this information?" you can often eliminate the concerns and highlight the blessing she brings to a setting.

While I will be covering this in more detail later, use the form from Appendix A to consider who might need to know some of this plan and information.

A PLACE TO BEGIN

As you look at the form from Appendix A, you now have this individual firmly in your mind. As we walk through the next sections of this book, remember that any ideas and plans you generate should come from your knowledge of this individual. We want to wrap our environment around this hand-crafted individual who has been made by God to fill an important spot in His kingdom. Instead of shoving this person into a "one size fits all" curriculum or class, let's design supports around this person so we can best reach and include this friend, child, sibling, or aging parent.

Sinking by Randy Beumer

ACCESSIBLE GOSPEL

God loves you very much and He wants you to be His child.

But there's a problem. We are not like God. We do wrong things, called sin, that keep us away from God.

But God has an idea! He loves us so much that He sent His son Jesus. Jesus took the punishment for our wrong things.

When we talk to God, believe His idea, and tell Him
- *"I'm sorry" for the wrong things I do*
- *"Thank you" for Jesus*
- *"I love you,"*

we become friends with God forever. We get to be God's child.

Yes, this is God's idea. God has made the way to Him accessible to all who believe. God opens His arms to people of all cultures, races, and ages. He longs to wrap His arms around males and females, as well as persons at all levels of ability. God is the one who established accessibility, and we get to bring that good news to the people in our lives. While the statements above can be worded in many different ways, that is the heart of the good news.

How do we take that good news to our grandchildren, children, friends, students, and congregation members who may learn and communicate a bit differently? Not only do we hope to SHOW those around us that our lives are transformed by Jesus, but how can we TELL about what Jesus has done? How do we communicate the depth of the love we have experienced and express that to our friend?

While the Holy Spirit is at work drawing people to God, and it's God who makes the connection in each heart, what tools can we use to tell about the good news of Jesus Christ? While I believe God will reveal His ideas to you, this section of the book looks at some stories and thoughts for you to consider as you pray about sharing the gospel and making these ideas most accessible to your friend.

INTRODUCTION

Imagine being the newly appointed mission coordinator to Thailand. You have eight weeks to prepare for your first trip to this country. What sort of things might you do to prepare for your visit and the opportunity to tell people about life in Jesus Christ? Perhaps your list would include such items as learning the language, understanding the culture, finding out what is important to people in that country, finding a key contact in Thailand who can be your guide, assembling a team of interested people, praying over this trip, and purchasing clothing that would be received well by the people of Thailand. You might also want to discover phrases or actions that would be considered rude or hurtful to those in Thailand. That's also part of creating open doors.

The analogy is clear. Now that we have a good understanding of our friend, it's time to apply that knowledge to creating an environment where we can share the good news of Jesus Christ. So often, we are the ones who are limited. We were taught how to present the gospel using a particular tool like the Romans Road. The Romans Road uses key verses in the book of Romans to explain the plan of salvation. While this has been helpful to many, it may have less appeal to a person for whom spoken words are not the first language. While the content is important, how we present that content may require some creativity and prayerful consideration. We may first need to learn to speak that individual's language, to find out that person's story and what that individual really enjoys. Perhaps we need to find that person's "expert" or "guide" so we can better form a safe and productive relationship. Have we considered creating a team that may include intercessors, or perhaps purchasing some items that would be well received by that person? Do we know what phrases to avoid with this individual?

While it's not possible to list one right way to set up the environment for presenting the gospel to your friend, I do want to share several stories that will get your creative juices flowing. When crafting an individualized plan, hearing what has been helpful in other situations can often lead to your own best idea to try. Remember, we are not the one who saves, that's God's part. But we are called to set up an environment where we can arrange an introduction.

JESSICA'S STORY

Jessica has an amazing puzzle piece. God has used her countless times to teach me and open my mind to things that exist in a spiritual realm. Jessica enjoys jokes and words. She loves to write stories, and she also enjoys cats. Her green areas are many as she is a hard worker and also is a loyal friend. Pink for Jessica would be some academic tasks and understanding the total picture of social relationships. She happens to have autism spectrum disorder.

Perhaps someday I will write a book just about Jessica. For this book, however, I want to tell you the story of Jessica saying "I love you" to Jesus. This particular morning at Zeeland Christian School was the culmination of many months of wrestling with the lies Jessica had chosen to believe. Children at another school had said that Christians have cooties. Being a very literal interpreter of language, Jessica walked far away from the things of Jesus given the comments of these other students. Even after transitioning to our Christian school, we stood beside Jessica's parents in battling these lies and the deep impact this had on her spiritually.

On February 29, however, we were together in a corner in my classroom. I had planned the materials and lesson based on my knowledge of the things that are important to Jessica. One of Jessica's strong interests was Star Trek. She could recite many parts of those episodes. Jessica enjoyed the variety of costumes and characters from that popular TV show. Jessica learned much better from concrete items and things you could touch. I also knew to be careful about using too many figures of speech from Christianity as this would be confusing to her. She is very literal in her understanding.

God's presence was clear as He led this conversation and activity. I had found a plastic set of armor based on the Scripture passage from Ephesians 6 that describes putting on the armor of God. I had set out the belt of truth, the shield of faith, the sword of the Spirit, and the other pieces in this child's play set. The helmet, however, I held on my lap. There was no script in my head, I just knew that Jessica did not yet have access to the helmet because it was the helmet of salvation. We had talked many times about Jesus and how we can belong to Him. Each time, she had chosen not to respond. I knew that I was using too many words with her. I needed something concrete.

Jessica started to dress up in the costume pieces. I explained what each item was. When she was nearly done, she asked for the helmet on my lap. I told her, "No, you can't have this part." Perhaps this sounds manipulative; even I had not planned these words out. Yet, it was soon clear how God would use this time together. I explained that this was the helmet of salvation. "You can wear this helmet when you understand and believe God's plan. God loves you very much, Jessica. He wants you to be His child, just like your mom and dad and Mrs. Newman are His children. But the wrong things we do called sin doesn't let us be close to God. That's why God sent Jesus to take our punishment instead of us. When you talk to God and tell Him that you are sorry for doing the things that make Him sad, that you love Jesus for taking your punishment, and that you want to be God's child, then you get to wear the helmet of salvation."

Right then, Jessica said, "I want to talk to God." She prayed a beautiful prayer and then I got to see something that has transformed not only Jessica, but me. For the first time, I got to witness the miracle of salvation in a person who has no social veil. She didn't wonder or check around and decide how she should look or act. I witnessed the Holy Spirit change her life. And it was instant. Never had I seen a life changed in front of my eyes in such immediate ways. As the Holy Spirit invaded Jessica, she had a new look on her face. While she used to be delighted with Star Trek, that was gone. She now was totally consumed with telling other people about Jesus. She obtained a cross that she wore around her neck. She would compare stories with people and talk about February 29 and wondered what date they became a Christian. She talked to people at school, at home, and on the bus. Jessica is a sister in Christ who continues to teach me. Her food for thought the other day was when she said, "My body has autism, but my spirit does not." While Jessica may have many meanings for this, I believe one of the things she was saying is that while she has the differences associated with autism, her connection with God is unhindered.

Was it the plastic armor set? Was it some creative manipulation that I held this helmet on my lap? Was it something in the date being February 29? No. It was God. The Holy Spirit invaded room 8 at Zeeland Christian School and used the humble tools available to draw her to Him and make that connection with Jessica. I was called to get to know Jessica and create an environment where I could make the introduction. But salvation is a gift from God – one that He has given me – and one that He poured out on Jessica that day. Now we both engage in the joy of introducing others to Jesus Christ. Just as God has dramatically changed both of our lives, He longs to invade the lives of others.

Are you ready to join Jessica and me on this mission? You have relationships with people we will never meet. God has put you in a unique position to reach certain individuals. Please take time to pray over this opportunity. It may be someone with a disability, or it could be someone who is your neighbor. When my son heard about this process of getting to know an individual and then making an environment where you can set up the best introduction between Jesus and this person, he noted that this really "works for everyone." How true.

SCOTT AND THE SUMMER CAMP: A REMINDER TO START BY GETTING TO KNOW THE INDIVIDUAL

Before we launch into additional ideas, I want to tell Scott's story. Like Jessica, Scott lives with autism spectrum disorder. I met Scott after a disastrous introduction to Jesus where he decided he wanted nothing to do with that church or anyone in it. One important thing to know about Scott and many others with ASD is that they often process language very literally. If you would happen to mention that it's "raining cats and dogs," that person would rush to the window to watch that happening if it's the first time that phrase was used.

If you think about it, many Christians use figurative language to describe a religious truth. Even Scripture uses some interesting analogies. Psalm 91:4 states, *He will cover you with His feathers, and under His wings you will find refuge; His faithfulness will be your shield and rampart.* To persons with ASD, this could be confusing. Does this make God a hen?

Imagine what happened one day when Scott was at summer camp retreat with the youth group from his church. While it was excellent that they included Scott with the other youth from church, the people in charge had not spent time really getting to know him. They skipped that part. One of the presenters made the call to the group. He mentioned that they could be "covered with the blood of Jesus" and then asked if anyone wanted to "give their heart to Jesus." Scott was absolutely in horror. This was like an R-rated horror movie in his head. He made a hasty exit and promised to never return. He was picturing people surgically removing their hearts and thick, red blood covering the place.

Thankfully, Scott is a willing learner. I wrote Scott a story about what those phrases really mean. After we gave him a new definition of those words, people can use those phrases with Scott now because he has the interpretation. Scott did, indeed, "give his heart to Jesus" and he is "covered with His blood." He is my brother in Christ and I am so thankful for him. He stands as an example today that we must begin by getting to know the individual. It would have saved Scott some trauma!

CAPTURE THE FLAG: REVISED

Greg, a young adult in my life, offers another story. Greg loves sports and camping. He enjoys moving and laughing. Spoken words are a struggle for Greg even though he understands many words. Greg has Down syndrome.

One summer, Greg was especially taken with a game at his summer camp called Capture the Flag. For the sake of this illustration, and for those who have not been camp counselors or youth group leaders, Capture the Flag is a game with two teams and a field or section of land that is divided into two halves by some sort of middle line or boundary. Each team gets 1 or more flags (sometimes a sock tied to a stick) to hide or place on their side of the playing field. Many teams appoint a few people to guard these flags for the duration of the game. On each side is also some sort of base that represents a "jail." The object of the game is to sneak across the field and try to capture the other team's flag or flags without getting tagged before you get back to your side. If you get tagged, then you must go to the jail. The only way to get free is to have a teammate sneak back across the field and tag you. Once you are tagged in the jail, you get a free walk back to your home team.

Since Greg was delighted with Capture the Flag, it seemed like a great tool when setting up an environment to make the introduction between Jesus and Greg. In a smaller space, I set up the middle line, a couple of flags, and a jail. Together, using movement and his love of this game, we talked about the flag on the other side trying to get us to do bad things – things that made God sad. Then, sin captured us and put us in jail. We stood together there and yelled out "Help! We are stuck! Get me out of this sin jail!" Even though my words were articulated more clearly than Greg's words, he understood what we were doing. Then I asked a friend to play the role of Jesus. I told Greg that if we ask Jesus to help, He will stay in jail for us and we can have a free walk back. Jesus came to earth to be in sin jail for us so we can have a free walk back. We gave Jesus a hug and then got to walk across the middle line. We cheered as Jesus later walked back over the line – knowing that Jesus is much stronger than sin and we get to be with Him on the Jesus side.

This environment made a big difference for Greg. He understood. In fact, he reenacted this Capture the Flag game several times for others. We knew what he was doing, and this game became a witness to many others who got to watch it. It was Greg's testimony.

Would this work with someone else? Possibly. But it was really important to notice Greg's love for this particular game and then turn it into a way to tell the gospel story. The Holy Spirit was at work drawing Greg and God used this environment to allow Greg to see His amazing love for him – and Greg responded!

NICOLE'S STORY: WE ARE RESPONSIBLE FOR CREATING THE ENVIRONMENT

As I was speaking at a conference in San Diego, I was on a panel of speakers to address this issue of spiritual formation and persons with disabilities. A mother raised her hand. "You are telling stories about people who can respond with actions and words. What about my daughter? Given the seizures she has, the psychologists say she will never be able to think or act past what a 6-month-old can do. What can I do to introduce my daughter to Jesus?" One of the speakers beat me to an answer. She told this mom that she does not need to do anything – that her daughter would be considered by God like an infant who dies. I struggled with this answer. This mom was not asking about what God would do. This mom wanted to know what SHE could do.

They entrusted me with the microphone and I asked that mom some questions. "What makes your daughter smile?" "What things does she like to do?" "What is her favorite toy?" It was clear that music was one of her favorite things. Since it's God's part to provide salvation, can we still create an environment for an introduction? The music team at this mom's church certainly thought that was true. After the conference, they made a recording of some songs that spoke Nicole's name as well as told about Jesus and His story. Playing this gave her a big smile on her face. In fact, they played these songs at Nicole's funeral. This mom and her congregation were faithful in creating an environment. How much more faithful is God in keeping His promises!

CLC NETWORK DRAMA TEAM: USE THE GIFTS OF EACH ONE

For many years I had the pleasure of directing a drama team. This was a team made up of actors with disabilities and some of their friends without disabilities. We visited many churches over the years and even enjoyed taking a bus tour one spring vacation. This particular drama was wordless. As the music played, the actors and actresses depicted Satan luring them into sin and capturing them. As they were tied up with scarves and trapped by a delighted Satan figure, Jesus came to them. He prayed over them and then the actors rose at Satan's signal and they started to nail Jesus to an imaginary cross. They laughed and mocked as they hammered with pretend tools until Jesus died. After spending some time under a grave cloth, Jesus rose in a great victory. To the tune of "Nothing but the Blood of Jesus," one by one the actors and actresses chose to leave the lure of sin and walked under a red cloth into the loving arms of Jesus. Jesus traded their scarves of sin for a colorful scarf representing freedom in Christ. The final scene showed these new believers holding out their scarves for those watching and inviting them into a life of freedom as a Christian.

As the director of this drama, I had the best seat in the house. Not only did I watch these actors and actresses fully practice the gospel message for their own lives, I got to see the impact the drama had on those watching. The person in the drama who played the part of Jesus was an amazing actor. His facial expression communicated volumes. His open arms of welcome looked inviting for everyone watching. His passionate and personal relationship with Jesus Christ came through clearly as he portrayed this role. He also happens to have Down syndrome.

As these children and adults performed the nine-minute drama, not only did people see the salvation message and what happened to the physical body of Christ, they also got to see a very visual reminder that the body of Christ, the Church, is made up of a variety of individuals. As those performing ministered to those watching, it was clear that people were moved. We often allowed others watching a chance to come under the red cloth and be welcomed into the arms of Christ. Several stories came back to us about this drama being the tool God used in the life of someone watching – an individual accepted the invitation to become a Christian.

I offer this story as an example of something you may be able to do in your own community. It's also a reminder to use the gifts of each one. Those in the drama were truly gifted and used by God in this way. The inclusive picture of friends ministering together is also something that spoke to those watching. Think of how you can use the green areas of each one, and how that might create avenues for practicing and spreading the gospel. In this case, some persons with disabilities and their friends were instrumental in bringing the gospel message to others while also experiencing the power of God's love in their own lives.

THE JOY OF BRAINSTORMING

As a speaker, I have had the joy of presenting this topic in many locations around the country. While I always hope to encourage and leave ideas for people to try, it's clear that I have been a learner too. One of my favorite parts of this session is asking participants to think about a particular individual, what they know about that person, and then what kind of ideas they may have in introducing this person to Jesus. Here is a list of great ideas that some are going to try:

Videos[1]

Finding Nemo is a favorite movie for Joey. His Sunday school teacher is going to use this with everyone in the class and create a parallel to the gospel message.

Beauty and the Beast has a transformation scene at the end. The one who created this portion of the movie is a Christian. It was designed to show the transformation that happens in giving our life to Jesus Christ. This is Amanda's favorite movie, so her mom wants to use this with her.

A church volunteer meets every week with a man with an intellectual disability. His friend loves *Star Wars*. They started to use this to understand the battle between God and Satan and he actually found a Bible study on the Internet that uses *Star Wars* as a base. This has been an excellent tool to better understand the gospel message.

One church volunteer noted an adult's continued interest in *The Adventures in Odyssey*.[2] She decided they would write a new episode together – one that highlights the salvation message.

As you watch a favorite movie with a friend, do you see any similarities with the gospel message? If so, this might be a tool you can use!

Bible apps and technology

You Version[3] is a Bible app available for download on many devices. In addition to materials for adults, they have an interactive and completely free set of Bible stories for children. You can find the material at bible.com/kids. One dad has spent hours beside his son as they interact around the life, death, and resurrection of Jesus. Dad uses this to allow his son Mark the chance to show others how to use the app and tell the story.

People have found great success by searching for some sort of online Bible study based around an area of interest. It's incredible what they have found. While you would still need to preview it and modify that resource, it's worth checking!

The technology person for a larger church is taken with Jason. It's unclear what Jason may understand, but he wants to put together a movie about Jesus and His love for Jason – and he wants to have Jason be in the movie. Jason lights up when he sees himself in a mirror, so he is thinking Jason would be drawn to this video.

Hands-on tools

Marta's grandma sees her love for instant hand sanitizer. She is planning on using that to talk about how Jesus is like that hand sanitizer. He comes to clean us up from our sins. She is even making up a special bottle so they can act it out together.

Jayger's Church school teacher sees his love for playing with cars. She is planning to make up the Jesus track. It will have a Jesus car wash and she wants to put Jayger's picture on one of the cars, get it dirty with sin, and then let Jayger run it through the Jesus wash. She is even thinking up a special song to use as they switch out that "sin car" with one that is clean and new.

Hayliegh has a love for butterflies. Her aunt and uncle want to set up a special butterfly collection that features the life cycle of a Christian. Their idea even involved a special poster at the end where Hayliegh could insert her picture into the cycle. As the brainstorming continued, they also were thinking of taking her favorite book – *The Very Hungry Caterpillar*[4] – and turning it into a story about the transformation that takes place in a person who loves and serves Jesus.

Jaylin loves Barbie dolls. Her creative dad is deciding they will use the Barbie dolls to act out the story of Jesus and how He loves us so very much. They can put on this show for several family members as Jaylin gets to hear and act out the story several times.

THE EASTER BOOK

If you are still looking for some printed resources and more ideas, I had the chance to write a book called *The Easter Book*[5] for Friendship Ministries. While I typically do not write curriculum, I was lured into the opportunity to come up with several pages of ideas for presenting the salvation story... without asking anyone to "give your heart to Jesus." While this book is part of a larger set of materials, it contains many activities you may be able to use, especially with adults. One of my favorite portions of the book is a fill-in-the-blank story that goes along with a bracelet. Each color on the bracelet matches up with a part of the explanation of becoming a Christian. The final project is a bracelet and story about that person giving his or her life to Jesus.

You can find *The Easter Book* at www.clcnetwork.org or at www.friendship.org

YOU TRY IT

I hope that your mind is already bubbling with ideas to try. Begin with the form you created from Appendix A. Look first at the puzzle piece on page 86. Focus on the green part of the puzzle piece that displays the gifts, strengths, and interests of that person. Those words should provide some of the first clues. Do you have words like music or drawing? Does your friend enjoy baking or playing games? As you study those words, does it bring up an avenue you may be able to use in your introduction of the good news of Jesus Christ?

The greens on the puzzle piece will often be the activity to house the message. If your adult friend enjoys baking, then you might make Easter rolls. When you break them open, they are hollow inside. You could find a recipe for a resurrection cake where each layer and part represents what Jesus has done for us. Turn the baking environment into an introduction to Jesus.

Perhaps you are a parent. If your child is "green" at playing and running, you might create a fitness course where each station tells a part of the story of God's love in Jesus Christ. Perhaps you are a grandparent and your grandchild enjoys playing board games with you. If that's a green part for your grandchild, how could you adapt his or her favorite board game to represent the parts of the gospel message?

Are you a youth group leader? Perhaps a green area for your teen is a particular sport. What about acting or playing drums? Consider those green areas as the activity to house the message.

Next, focus on the ways your friend takes information in. Do you have notes on Appendix A about the importance of using pictures or keeping it short due to attention span? Can you use books with words or would you want to use music? How a person takes information in will help you choose the content for the activity. For example, if you are doing the Easter cake baking, should you have a word recipe or picture recipe to describe the gospel layers of the cake?

As you look at ways your friend gets information out, this will be the way you can check for understanding. For example, if your friend can pull you to a particular place and you are doing the fitness course, you could ask your friend to take you to the place that shows us Jesus is alive. If your friend can point to a picture or object and you are doing a board game, have that person point to someone that Jesus loves in order to move forward 4 spaces.

As you plan your environment and activity, make sure to factor in movements, sensory sensitivities, safety issues, and equipment needed. For example, if you are interacting with a person who is green in throwing a ball, you might choose some sort of game format. But if that individual has sensitive ears and you bring balloons into the game, that individual may not want to engage in the activity.

As the activity begins to form in your mind, consider constructing the content so that you can repeat it and review it. Having a fitness course means that you can do the stations many times over. Having a picture recipe that goes along with the cake gives you a way to look at that recipe together and remember the cake-baking experience. Doing a drama or creating a chant to the drum rhythm is something you can record and watch together later. Creating something lasting allows you to come back to it and learn from it many times over.

And take it from a special education teacher, your very first idea will most likely need to be altered, tweaked, modified, or even scrapped. In the time I spent with Jessica, the armor of God idea was several ideas away from where we started. I watched her reaction each time, prayed for guidance, and God gave me more ideas for how to approach setting up a great environment where I could introduce her to the Lord of my life.

At this point, if nothing comes to mind, ask another individual to brainstorm with you. Remember to cover this process with prayer. God hand-crafted this individual and knows this person from before birth. Ask Him to highlight a path. Remember, you create the environment for the introduction to Jesus and His love for this individual, and watch God do the rest!

If you want to brainstorm or ask us to pray with you, please contact the CLC Network Church Services Division. We could have no greater joy than to come alongside you as you bring the good news of Jesus Christ to someone in your life. Prayer partners are standing by! E-mail info@clcnetwork.org.

Bless You by Kyle Ragsdale

INCLUSIVE WORSHIP

INTRODUCTION

Salvation – is it the beginning or the end? Once we step into that new place of belonging in Christ, what is next? Most people involved in evangelism are quick to comment that evangelism and discipleship walk hand in hand. Once we are a child of God, it's so important to put ourselves in places where God can continue the transformation in our lives.

2 Corinthians 3:18 says, *And we all, who with unveiled faces contemplate the Lord's glory, are being transformed into His image with ever-increasing glory, which comes from the Lord, who is the Spirit.*

While God can choose many ways and places to transform our lives, Christians usually place themselves strategically so they can hear God's voice and grow in Him. In my own life, I find being part of a church, a Christian small group, and finding daily time to spend by myself in God's presence are some things He has used to allow me to grow throughout my years as a follower of Jesus.

For our brothers and sisters in Christ who experience areas of disability, are those same avenues available? Can an individual with Down syndrome, for example, walk into any Christian church and find a place of welcome? Would an individual with autism spectrum disorder be able to find a small group that encouraged his participation? If talking to God and listening for His voice was not modeled or taught in large or small group settings, would it be easy for that same individual to know how to have a personal time with God each day?

While I know some persons with disabilities have found places of worship that are welcoming and meaningful, I know from many personal experiences and contacts that this is often not the case. It is my hope that God will use the practical ideas that follow to give churches and family members ideas to try when creating such environments.

THREE TYPES OF STORIES

I hear so many stories. They tend to fall into three categories:

"We are so excited!" The excited stories tend to be from communities already experiencing inclusive worship. They tell about the day Holly joined the praise team and how her ability to use signs and gestures instead of words allowed God to create a new and vibrant place for all to worship. The stories recount the day Mario was baptized and the powerful and positive impact that made on the church education program. The stories reference ministering with, worshiping with, and serving with persons with disabilities and how the church has changed as a result.

For churches with those types of stories, may God use this book to give you additional ideas.

"We really have not thought much about this in our church." I hear this many times from pastors and church members who fall into a second group of stories. I don't consider this a negative comment, but one that invites discovery. I often encourage these communities to remember that around 20 percent of our population experiences some kind of disability. That's a lot of people! Translated into a church setting, about one in every five people may need something altered or modified to be more a part of the community. It might be a hymnal in Braille, a rocking chair in the worship center, a hearing loop in the sanctuary, or a gluten free bread option for communion. That's a large number of people, so it's important for churches to consider what might need to happen in order to better welcome each one.

For churches with those kinds of stories, may God use this material to invite you into a place where you can consider some new options within your community. I am confident your stories will soon reflect the "I'm so excited" stories.

The third group of stories can best be summed up with **"We are not interested."** This set of stories, unfortunately still so prevalent, often tells of families who have knocked on many church doors only to be asked to leave. Other individuals might be sent to the church down the road as "I heard they have a program for people like you." Some families have become so tired and weary of searching for a church that they have given up and figure there is no spot for them within that community. Some parents go to church, but are always asked to shadow their family member with a disability in worship and educational settings. I often refer to these parents as some of the most "worship deprived" individuals in a church. Sometimes after years of filling this role, the families make a choice to stay home – it's just easier that way.

These stories are troubling, and yet when one begins to ask more questions, the reasons for these comments are often based in fear, inexperience, or a legitimate comment – "We want to include this person, but we don't know HOW."

For churches with those kinds of stories, may God use this material to give you the "how to" and address the fear and inexperience that often undergird these comments. Be bold, pray into this, and allow God to lead.

ACCESSIBLE CONVERSATION WITH GOD

Accessibility. I used that word to help us think about the gospel message. How do we make that more accessible to each one? Now imagine accessibility in church, a small group setting, and individual settings. While it's easy to think about issues like bathrooms, ramps, drinking fountains, pew cut outs for wheelchair users, and elevators, walk with me more deeply into this concept.

Most of our worship settings can be described as a conversation. While some of them are corporate and others are individual, we enter into a place where we speak to God and allow God to speak to our lives. For some individuals with disabilities, the tools we use as part of that conversation might be a bit different from some of the traditional tools. For example, if we use only spoken words set to music for the part of the conversation that says "I love you, God," then we have left someone out who has no spoken words. How can we make that part of our conversation with God inclusive of each worshipper?

While drinking fountains and bathrooms are very important, the focus of this book will be on the tools and techniques one might use in including persons with intellectual disability, autism spectrum disorder, or physical challenges that might prevent the use of more traditional tools in a worship setting. If, however, your congregation has not had the chance to look at your physical property, I recommend beginning with www.crcna.org/disability and click on the link for the accessibility audit guide.[1]

CONCEPT OF VERTICAL HABITS

Tom and Sally have been thrilled since they first knew that they would have a child. They prepared a safe and comfortable place for the baby to sleep, and their friends gave gifts of clothing, warm blankets and stuffed animals. And finally baby Asher arrived. They can hardly believe that this child was entrusted to them. They have prayed that the child would be healthy, would grow, and would come to love God as they do.

Before Asher can begin to understand, Tom and Sally are practicing habits of relating. They smile at him, talk to him, sing, laugh and quickly respond to his every need. Over and over they repeat "I love you." Their deepest desire is that a deep and loving bond will grow between Asher and them, their family, friends and God.

Their love is expressed not only in words but in actions. They eagerly watch for smiles from Asher that are a response to their love. As Asher grows they begin to teach him expressions that will help these bonds grow.

It would be three years before Tom and Sally receive the diagnosis that Asher has autism spectrum disorder. Though these years have been filled with frustration and uncertainty, they have been reminded that God loves Asher and desires to have a relationship with him. They know that God wants Asher to be deeply connected with his parents, siblings, and family and friends who love him.

As Asher grows they want to help him learn to express "Thank you" either in words or gestures. When he is older they'll teach him the importance of "I'm Sorry" and "Please help."

Asher, as is true for all of us, also needs to learn practices of relating to God. In many Christian churches, worship is shaped by these practices. In 2005 Dr. John Witvliet of the Calvin Institute of Christian Worship taught this concept in a workshop in Denver. Bruce Gritter and Karen Wilk, church planters in Edmonton, Alberta wondered whether this might help new believers understand why we do what we do in worship. Thinking of human relationships as horizontal and relating to God as vertical, they called it "Vertical Habits" and spent a year learning and practicing 8 habits.

After receiving their reports and resources, Calvin Institute of Christian Worship staff wondered,

> Would this framework be effective in congregations filled with life-long Christians?
>
> Might Christian schools shape faith formation using the Vertical Habits?
>
> Would it be meaningful in churches of various ethnicities and worship practices?

Twenty-three churches and schools accepted an invitation to learn about Vertical

Initial Vertical Habits Partners:

African Community Fellowship, Christian Reformed Church
Grand Rapids, MI

Bethlehem Church
Randolph, NJ

Clifton Baptist Church
Louisville, KY

College Hill Presbyterian Church
Louisville, KY

Cornerstone Christian Reformed Church
Ann Arbor, MI

Covenant Life Church
Grand Haven, MI

Crossroads Community Church
Schererville, IN

Daybreak Community Church
Valparaiso, IN

Drayton Christian Reformed Church
Drayton, Ontario, Canada

Friends of the Groom
Terrace Park, OH

Midland Park Christian Reformed Church
Midland Park, NJ

Monroe Community Church
Grand Rapids, MI

New Life Church
New Lenox, IL

River City Church
Cambridge, Ontario, Canada

Sojourn Community Church
Louisville, KY

St. Luke's Lutheran Church
Grand Rapids, MI

St. Thomas Episcopal Church
Terrace Park, OH

The River Community Church
Edmonton, Alberta, Canada

Third Christian Reformed Church
Zeeland, MI

Trinity Reformed Church
Orange City, IA

Tualatin Presbyterian Church
Tualatin, OR

United Theological Seminary
Dayton, OH

Unity Christian High School
Hudsonville, MI

Habits and practice them for a year. At the end of the year they shared resources and reflections.

I also had a chance to work with the Vertical Habits project. My role was to consider how this language, this new way of looking at elements of a worship service and growing as a Christian, might impact the life of a person with a disability. There was such beauty in the way large words like "adoration," "confession," or "prayer for illumination" could be looked at much more simply. "Love you," "Sorry," and "I'm listening" often make more sense not only to new Christians but also to those with more concrete vocabularies. In fact, Vertical Habits impacted my conversation with God as well.

In addition, I had learned as a special educator that repetition is really important for my students. Practicing the same concept in a variety of ways was pivotal to learning new concepts. The same would be true for growing as a Christian. In that way, the use of the word "habit" was also a delight for me. In order to think about the topic of Christian or spiritual formation, the idea of building habits of saying "I love you" to God seemed really important. This vocabulary could be practiced in corporate settings, but also at home before bedtime.

As I looked more deeply into the concept of Vertical Habits, it not only made sense in allowing a person with a disability to enter into worship and grow as a Christian, it also seemed to be a common denominator for all who are worshippers of Jesus Christ. Vertical Habits, therefore, opened the doors to inclusive worship opportunities – a place where all believers can practice these habits and words together.

Since launching this project, many churches, schools, and families have found that the Vertical Habits help both adults and children grow in their relationship with God. In fact, it's become the structure CLC Network uses when suggesting ideas for Christian formation and including persons with disabilities in corporate worship settings. Other names have sometimes been used to describe the process such as "Created to Worship" and "Growing Towards God." The Psalms provide a biblical guide to shape the process both in worship and in relationships. Churches, schools, and individuals that use Vertical Habits say it helps develop worship habits that deepen their relationship with God and affect every part of their lives. A school which recently spent a year with Vertical Habits reported, "We will never be the same."

VERTICAL HABITS AT A GLANCE

Love You	I'm Sorry	Why?	I'm Listening	Help	Thank You	What Can I Do?	Bless You
(Praise)	(Confession)	(Lament)	(Illumination)	(Petition)	(Gratitude)	(Service)	(Blessing)

WHY HABITS ARE IMPORTANT

We teach children to brush their teeth regularly so that as they grow it becomes a habit. We teach children to say thank you so that any time someone does something kind for them they respond with gratitude. Helping children and adults develop habits in their relationship with God will help them grow throughout their lives.

These habits can shape our response to a sunset or a siren. We can give thanks to God for the beautiful colors in the sky. We might offer a prayer of protection for the stranger whose life is changed by some trauma that requires the response of the emergency vehicle. Vertical Habits can help people of all ages and abilities develop habits that will point them to God in the circumstances of everyday life. And in so doing, faith is shaped and strengthened.

In the following pages you will find each Vertical Habit that becomes part of our worship conversation with God and therefore part of our Christian Formation. Each Vertical Habit comes with suggestions of how the habit can be taught and practiced during worship that takes place in church, school, small group, and individual times. While we will offer many practical tools on how you can include each individual, you will want to adapt the concepts for your unique context and for those you are including. Be creative. Remember to begin by getting to know the individuals you are including and find out what that person CAN do.

Appendix C is filled with additional ideas generated by the school and churches involved in this Vertical Habits project. Adapt, use, enjoy.

LOVE YOU (PRAISE)

Sing praises to God, sing praises;
Sing praises to our King, sing praises,
For God is the King of all the earth;
Sing to Him a Psalm of Praise.
Psalm 47:6-7

People experience God's love expressed through the love of family, teachers, pastors, and friends. Children, for example, enjoy responding to love and expressing their love by drawing a picture of a flower or a rainbow. A hug expresses love without words. And often a warm smile says "I love you" more deeply than words.

Saying "I love you" to God is part of most worship experiences. Whether in a large group or as an individual moving through his or her daily routine, it's important to give people the opportunity to express love to God. While much of this is done through spoken words or words set to music, consider additional ways to convey those words.

Learning from a story

Christmas Day at my former church congregation was one of my favorite worship services. At the end of the service, they would invite people to come forward and sing the Hallelujah Chorus. I would proudly join the alto section, ready to be thrilled by the music and the text.

Three days before Christmas I hunted down my copy of Handel's *Messiah*. I was ready. Two days before Christmas I came down with the sniffles. "No big deal," I thought. "It's only the sniffles." By Christmas morning, however, I had no voice. It was gone. I might have been able to sing the bass line, but the alto line was out of the question. Not only would I not be able to sing the Hallelujah Chorus, I was going to have to sit out of all the Christmas carols lined up for that morning as well. I remember thinking that I might as well stay home that Christmas Day, and that's exactly what ended up happening.

Many years later, I look on that day as a powerful lesson from God. For a moment in time, I was given the opportunity to know what it is like to be one of my friends who is unable to use language as part of a worship service. Perhaps from a physical difference or some type of intellectual disability, some participants are unable to utter words or songs of praise to God each and every day. My lack of creativity as well as my disobedience on that Christmas Day is overwhelming to me now. Psalm 150:6 says, *Let everything that has breath praise the Lord. Praise the Lord.* The Bible is clear – if you are breathing, you need to be offering praise to God. Singing is one way to do that, but some individuals need to be creative in their praise to God each and every day.

While Psalm 150 ends with the words, *Everything that has breath praise the Lord*, the rest of the Psalm reminds me of some type of idea bank. The Psalmist suggests tambourines, cymbals (even loud ones), dancing, strings, and much more. In fact, singing isn't even mentioned in this Psalm. What is very clear, however, is that God is worthy of praise, and there are many ways to focus your heart on Him and let Him know. As hard as it was for me to comprehend on that Christmas Day, I had many options available to me. What I lacked was a focused and grateful heart.

Praising God is not optional for Christians. Why, then, do we often offer such limited methods of doing that in our worship services? Saying "I love you" to God is on each heart, not only on the hearts of those who have a voice to speak it forth.

Similar to Psalm 150, the list that follows is an idea bank. Remember, don't look at what an individual CAN'T do; look for what that person CAN do to praise God. As God has designed each person, it makes sense that He also designed each person to be able to praise Him and follow the expectations laid out for us in Scripture. If singing is not on the list, what options are available and how can you incorporate that into your worship service or personal times of worship? No one is off the hook. If you are breathing, you need to participate. If you are planning the worship service, you need to provide each participant with the opportunity.

Idea Bank for "Love You" (Praise):

1. Teach some basic signs and gestures to your congregation. Many children's curricula as well as curriculum for persons with disabilities use movements with the words. Although one cannot call these movements "sign language," which adheres to a very strict grammatical structure for those who are deaf, using some signs and gestures often enhances the meaning of the text. For example, the sign for Jesus is a tactile reminder of the nails that went into the hands of our Savior. If I had known the sign for "Hallelujah" on my voiceless Christmas morning, I could have participated in a new way, giving expression to my love for Jesus. I can say "Love you" to Jesus with sign at other times in the service

as well. Perhaps the entire congregation can learn the sign for "Love you," and use it after prayer times, praise times, or at times of commitment. The Internet is rich with resources that could demonstrate signs and gestures that can be paired with words.

2. Create some banners, flags, praise rings, and other items individuals can use to praise God. Waving a wrist ribbon in place of, or in addition to, singing can be a colorful way to show praise to God. Directions for a variety of visual praise instruments can be found in a resource called *The Easter Book*[1]. Written as part of the curriculum for Friendship Ministries, this book contains instructions for making many items. Children's educational supply catalogs also offer pre-made ribbons and flags in the music section.

3. If you are in a setting where you allow participants to choose songs, try putting together a song selection board. Either with pictures or words, make up a set of index-sized cards that allow a person who is not verbal to go forward and point to or pick up a song that the whole group will be singing.

4. Some individuals may be without voice and without much movement. In some cases, you may be able to drape a wheelchair with ribbons of praise and have a person push that wheelchair around the group, allowing the ribbons or flags to surround the congregation. (Make sure you first get permission from the wheelchair user to do this!) The color of the flag or ribbons may also be tied in to the song or message. If one, for example, is singing about the blood of Jesus covering our sins, as the red flag passes each person it is a reminder of the sacrifice and love of Jesus. The individual in the wheelchair, therefore, is not an added extra or exhibit, but a meaningful part of the worship experience for all involved.

5. In some cases, the time of singing and praise can be painful to certain individuals. Primarily for those with auditory sensitivity (where a sound that might be at just the right volume level to most, is painfully loud to a few individuals), churches may need to provide creative ways to mute the sounds so that the person can relax and participate. Some hardware stores sell sound blocking devices used in construction work. These can be very helpful for individuals who need to block out some of the sound during worship. At times, earmuffs or headphones can do that as well. Some individuals may prefer to engage in singing time in the cry room or other room where the volume can be turned down to a comfortable level. The person may then join others for the remainder of the worship service. (For more information on auditory differences and other sensory areas, read the book *Autism and Your Church: Nurturing the Spiritual Growth of People with Autism Spectrum Disorder*[2]. In this book, I have given several additional adjustments for those who experience sensory differences).

6. Some individuals without speech also have a communication device. It might be a paper board with pictures or a computer that is operated by pushing buttons. Talk to the individual or the individual's caregiver. It might be possible to program that device to include some things the individual might be able to contribute in a worship setting. For example, one might place 3-4 song selections on that board for the individual to choose. One might put the phrase "love you" on that board so that the individual can select that to say to God. In my experience, teens are often masters at technology. If the individual has other people program the device, teach a couple of teens to operate it so that the individual can respond based on what material or questions are being asked.

7. Ultimately, each one of us needs a chance to make a commitment to accept Jesus as Savior for the first time. Many church settings offer a chance for participants to do just that. If one only allows for a verbal option, some would be unable to participate. Consider having some paper hearts available that can be tailored with the individual's name. Instead of telling Jesus "love you," one could place a heart with the individual's name by a cross or other designated area. Another option would be to teach the signs for "love you" and allow people to speak or sign that as a commitment to Jesus. Think broadly when you give an invitation to accept Christ. Are you being inclusive of all those represented?

8. "Everyone please stand to sing" is a common phrase we use in our worship settings. If someone is unable to stand, it would make more sense to say, "Please stand in body or in spirit." That way all can participate.

9. This idea bank is only a way to get your own creative juices flowing. Put yourself in the shoes of the individual in your congregation with a disability. If the person is not able to speak, then you try not speaking for a service. What options do you see as one who cannot speak? If the person is unable to use their arms and legs, then you try it for a service. What options do you see? Create those options in large and small group settings and be open to having God use the actions of that individual to touch your congregation in ways you never thought were possible.

I'M SORRY (CONFESSION)

Generous in love – God give grace!
Huge in mercy – wipe out my bad record.
Scrub away my guilt, soak out my sins in your laundry.
I know how bad I've been; my sins are staring me down.
You're the one I've violated, and you've seen it all,
seen the full extent of my evil.
You have all the facts before you;
whatever you decide about me is fair.
Psalm 51:1-4 (The Message)

For both adults and children, confession is difficult. Why do you think this is true? It is hard to acknowledge we have done wrong, that we have hurt someone, that we have responded or acted in anger. But for a healthy relationship with God and with the people in our lives, honest confession is essential. Openly recognizing what we have done and expressing our regret allows us to move forward in healing a relationship. Adults can model confession in their speech with each other, with their children, and in talking with God.

The Bible is filled with assurances that God desires our confessions and promises forgiveness. Adults can demonstrate forgiveness when a child confesses he has done wrong, even though there may be consequences for the action. Expressing love even when someone has disappointed or hurt us demonstrates God's grace toward all of us.

During worship, churches have a variety of ways to help worshipers confess their sins to God. In some churches this is a regular part of every worship service, along with an assurance of God's forgiveness. In other churches confession is mentioned only rarely, often because they assume that people are uncomfortable talking about sin. Christians who regularly confess their sins to God and to one another express that the freedom that comes with confession leads to renewed love and praise. Each individual, then, needs a chance to say "I'm sorry" in an inclusive worship setting.

Learning from a story

This vertical habit gives us a chance to examine our own lives and congregations through the eyes of a family with a child with autism spectrum disorder. The parents were delighted in the child's progress. The young boy had made great gains in Kindergarten. He was cherished by his peers who cheered him on for each new word he could use. As the parent-teacher conference was coming to a close, I asked, "Does Henry enjoy Church school?" They looked at each other and then started to reveal a three-year nightmare. Like all of the other children who turn 3, Henry's parents took him to Church school. After the hour was over, a very tired teacher took Henry back to his parents and said, "Please don't ever bring Henry back to Church school." Unprepared for a child with autism spectrum disorder, the teacher felt she had no other response. Taking this to heart, the parents took turns staying home with Henry. By the time I asked them this question at conferences, it had been three years since they had worshiped together as a family. A call to the pastor, a few strategies for the Church school staff, and now the family is firmly embedded in their congregation.

How many individuals with disabilities have a similar story? I have heard hundreds. A place that should represent inclusion and healing is often the source of pain and rejection. Our churches often have willing hearts, but they don't always feel as though they have the expertise. God's expectation, however, is very clear. 1 Corinthians 12:21 says, *The eye cannot say to the hand, 'I don't need you!' And the head cannot say to the feet, 'I don't need you!'* Have we done this in our church community? Have we sent some away? Have we been inclusive or exclusive?

It appears to me that this vertical habit of confession, saying "I'm sorry" to God, may need to begin with our response to God's command to live as an inclusive body of Christ. Are you a church community that reflects the amazing diversity that God wove into His body, or are you a community that has been unwilling to make accommodations for those who need them? Have you sent children and youth away from your Church school and youth group? Have you placed barriers for adults who wish to attend your worship service? Perhaps the best place to begin a new path is on our knees – saying "I'm sorry" to God for our disobedience in this area. Make a new commitment to echo God's heart: *Now you are the body of Christ, and each one of you is a part of it.* 1 Corinthians 12:27

Prayer of Confession: Lord, I am sorry. For lack of trusting you for the answers, I have been disobedient to your command to cherish each person in the body of Christ. For the hurt and damage I have done to another member of my family and your body, I am sorry. Teach me your new way. In the name of Jesus, Amen.

Idea Bank for "I'm Sorry" (Confession)

1. Ultimately, in addition to telling God, "Love you," we must also tell God, "I'm sorry." Once again, some individuals with disabilities will need this concept made more concrete. One way to do that is to select some type of coat or shirt. Put sticky-sided Velcro on the clothing item. Cut out a variety of "puddles" from gray cloth. Put the soft-sided Velcro on the back of those pieces and adhere them to the clothing. Talk about our sin – the things that make God sad – as having dirty mud stuck to us. When we tell Jesus "I'm sorry" for the things that make God sad, and when we say "Love you" to Jesus, He takes those muddy things off from us. Only people with clean clothes can be with God. Allow people to tell God "I'm sorry" and "Love you." Remove the mud.

2. A way to allow people to say "I'm sorry" without words can come in a chain and scarf exchange. By using a length of chain or mud-colored scarf, drape that around the neck of the individuals involved. Allow that person to come to an area with a cross or another designated spot to tell God "I'm sorry" by letting Him remove the chain. By telling God, "Love you," you receive a clean scarf in its place. You are now part of His family!

3. Once we have said, "I'm sorry" for the first time, there is still the need to recognize we live in a fallen world. One important thing to remember is that just as we need to be understanding with the actions of others, it's NOT OK to allow an individual with a disability to continue in sin, excusing it as "they can't help it." We may need to be understanding, loving, patient, and more, but just as you would confront another member of God's family, it's OK to expect godly living from an individual with a disability. I often do a workshop called "Heads – Promoting Acceptance, Tails – Encouraging Change." Not only do we need to promote acceptance of an individual on the part of others, we also need to encourage change and growth in the life of that individual. One child with Down syndrome was behaving very badly in Church school – showing a lot of disrespect to the teacher and other children. The leader had decided that it was OK because you couldn't expect more out of the child. I suggested that it's not OK to allow that child to go on "sinning." By putting some other parameters and supports in place, that child could grow and be more accepted by peers as well as exhibit more godly behavior in response to authority.

4. Perhaps because of our fallen nature, one of the very first phrases we teach our young children is "I'm sorry." We expect them to say that when they have wronged another individual. Presenting the concept of "sorry" to a person with a disability may need to begin with real-life practice. Do some role-playing with situations appropriate to individuals that age. Then apply that to our relationship with God. Just as we say "I'm sorry"

to our friend after we hurt him, we can tell God "I'm sorry" too. It made his friend feel happy; it makes God happy too.

5. Teach the sign for "I'm sorry" to your congregation. As a routine in your worship service, allow people to sign and say "I'm sorry" during times of confession.

6. Let people express "I'm sorry" by bowing or kneeling. If appropriate, let them know that God put His words of "I forgive you" in the pastor's hand or the leader's hand for right now. When they feel you touch the shoulders or head, it's like God saying, "I forgive you."

7. Allow opportunity for your whole congregation to say "I'm sorry" to God for not supporting an inclusive environment for those with unique gifts and needs. Preach a sermon, ask for testimonies, invite a special speaker, inform the congregation of God's expectation. Let the community say "I'm Sorry" and then allow God's Spirit to move in your community as you follow His commands.

Additional ideas for community awareness can be found in *Helping Kids Include Kids with Disabilities*[1] by Barbara J. Newman. *Your Feet, My Shoes*[2] by Sarah Bolt, the *Inclusion Awareness Kit*[3] by Barbara J. Newman, and *Body Building: Devotions to Celebrate Inclusive Community*[4] by Barbara J. Newman would also help children and adults in your community be more understanding and welcoming.

©Matt Hale

WHY? (LAMENT)

How long, Lord? Will you forget me forever?
How long will you hide your face from me?
How long must I wrestle with my thoughts and day after day
have sorrow in my heart?
How long will my enemy triumph over me?
But I trust in your unfailing love, my heart rejoices in your salvation.
I will sing the Lord's praise, for He has been good to me.
Psalm 13:1-2, 5-6

Sometimes children ask "Why?" so often that we grow weary of answering. Sometimes we can't answer because we don't know why. Our lives are filled with experiences we don't understand – a broken marriage, a crushing diagnosis, a miscarriage, death of a loved one, or life-changing damage to a previously healthy body. Why, Lord? We pray and pray without seeing any healing.

Sometimes in our relationship with God and in our churches we are afraid to ask God these hard questions. Expressing our anger with God because of what has brought us this pain seems inappropriate, even sinful.

But the Bible is filled with people who brought their pain and anger to God. We can be assured that God wants us to express our deepest emotions to Him. We can model this with others by allowing them to express their frustrations and anger to us.

Throughout the Psalms we find examples of people asking God hard questions. But every time they finally recognize God's love for them, even when circumstances don't change. Throughout the Bible we discover that the acknowledgement of pain leads to rebirth and new life.

Church leaders who include opportunities for lament in worship help the congregation acknowledge that they can bring their pain to God. This is counter-cultural in our American lifestyle where we try to pretend that our lives are happy and fulfilling. But there is much in our personal lives and in this broken world that brings us pain. We must be given permission and expression to ask God "Why, Lord?"

Learning from a story

He truly is a miracle. He wasn't expected to live past the first few days of his life. Jordan was born with bones the consistency of sawdust and a condition known as Osteogenesis Imperfecta (Brittle Bone Disease). Changing a diaper would break his bones, and he was carried around on a pillow to prevent injury. God's plan for Jordan's life was different than the plan of the doctor. He not only lived to see his first birthday, but he is fully alive today and very much a high school graduate. He still has brittle bones, lots of risks and injuries, but those who know Jordan realize he is a vibrant part of God's body.

As we talk to friends and family who know Jordan, it's clear that Jordan is a miracle. You don't only read the Bible to understand miracles, you can know Jordan's story and realize that God is active today in doing miracles. This is the truth.

It is also the truth that Jordan's siblings had a very unfortunate event one summer. After many issues with his health, they were able to go to the theme park Cedar Point, where Jordan's disability allowed them a fast trip to the front of the lines. Unfortunately, at the start of the day, Jordan's wheelchair tipped over, and he had another broken bone or two. The siblings knew that it was the right thing to do to leave with Jordan and head for the hospital. The siblings know that Jordan is loved by God and is a miracle. They also know how to ask that important question of God, "Why?" Why did Jordan have to break a bone today? Why do we have to say good-bye to mom so many days as she heads out with Jordan for treatments? Why do our needs go on hold so much of the time just to keep Jordan alive? Why does he have to hurt so much? Why don't the treatments make him all the way better? Why? How long? Although the brain knows the ultimate truth of God, the heart is quickly drawn into the everyday experience – and we ask "Why?"

One of the blessings of the inclusive school setting where I teach is that we have many siblings of individuals who have disabilities. Sometimes they lament together. Sometimes the siblings compare notes of trips that were cancelled, restaurants they had to leave, stares of passing people, conditions of brothers and sisters. It's OK to lament. It's OK to ask "Why?"

It's also important to have people there to finish the Psalm of Lament. It's important to experience the community of Christ with people who can state the truth. Psalm 13 ends with:

> But I trust in your unfailing love, my heart rejoices in your salvation.
> I will sing the Lord's praise, for He has been good to me.

When all the questions have been asked, it's important to return to the truth of what we know.

With Jordan and his family, we echo the questions of "Why?' and "How long?" We know that Brittle Bone Disease stinks, and we also question why the family's trip had to end that way one summer. We also join hands with you, praising God for His miracle in Jordan, and we give our strong testimony, "But I trust in your unfailing love."

Idea Bank for "Why?" (Lament)

1. Done with the permission of the individual or individual's family, sometimes it's helpful to hear a person's story. Hopefully hearing Jordan's story allows the issue of lament to become more understandable. Hopefully hearing Jordan's story also encourages us to speak God's truth about who Jordan is and where our hope lies. Many individuals with disabilities have a powerful testimony. Sometimes it's a miracle. Sometimes it's the opportunity to hear about a person who asked "Why?" many days and can now give powerful testimony to God's work in her life. Using a newsletter, bulletin insert, or testimony time, telling an individual's story can be a powerful way to better understand the whole concept of lament.

2. Many Psalms are considered a lament. Sometimes one can pick out a phrase that is repeated or inserted into a Psalm. Teach the signs and short phrase. As you read the Psalm, have the congregation speak or sign the repetitive phrase throughout the reading.

3. Teach the sign for "Why?" Let the congregation use that sign during this portion of the service.

4. Have a picture of an eye, an ear, and a brain. Let people talk about what they see and hear. Perhaps after a natural disaster or a congregational event of sadness, talk about the experience of what you see and hear. Then talk about what you know to be true about God. Talk about His love, His plan, His hope. Put that under the brain picture. It's OK to talk about what we see and hear, but it's also important to talk about what we know.

5. Put a small dumbbell in each hand. In one hand talk about the experience of what happened (the sadness, the event). Raise that dumbbell. Then raise the other one and talk about who God is – what you know to be true. Do these exercises, realizing that you need to change the weight of what you know to a bigger size. Despite what we experience, what we know about God is stronger and bigger.

6. Have people create a visual image or collage of current events that make us wonder about "Why?" this happened. When the collage is complete, place the phrase "I put my hope in God" or other similar Scripture that allows us to see that God's hope and His truth cover the events.

7. Although a visual collage is helpful, you might be able to use an individual for this activity. As a person shares their situation and people respond

with a time of joining in asking "Why?," have congregation members write God's truth on sticky-notes and place it on and around that individual or family.

8. Many times people with disabilities have hurts and questions that run very deep. After leading people through freedom appointments as outlined by Neil Anderson in *The Bondage Breaker: Overcoming Negative Thoughts, Irrational Feelings, Habitual Sins*,[1] it's clear to me that we can get stuck in the questions and never move on to the statements of truth and hope. As you allow people to share their hurts, fears, and disappointments, be prepared to listen and speak God's truth over them. It's in that reality that we as Christians get to live. It's in that place that we can experience God's peace even in difficult times. Give that gift to those in our community who struggle with issues of body and mind. It will be healing ointment for the soul!

I'M LISTENING (ILLUMINATION)

How can those who are young keep their way pure?
By living according to your word.
I seek you with all my heart;
Do not let me stray from your commands.
I have hidden your word in my heart
that I might not sin against you.
I meditate on your precepts and consider your ways.
I delight in your decrees; I will not neglect your word.
Psalm 119:9-11, 15-16

When we are talking with children we might ask, "Are you listening to me?" We are aware that when minds wander, instructions may not be heard with any accuracy. Sometimes in talking with other adults, we might be tempted to ask, "Are you listening?" Only with listening can there be a healthy relationship. Finding ways to capture your child's attention is probably something that has already been part of your role as a parent.

God tells us that it is important that we listen to Him. His word gives instruction for our relationship with Him and with others. In Psalm 119 we are reminded of the importance of having Scripture in our hearts that will shape all our decisions and actions.

In some churches there is prayer before Scripture asking God to open our hearts and minds to what God is saying to us. It turns out that children are not the only ones who have wandering minds. Adults, too, must be reminded of the importance of listening to God and to each other.

We live in a noisy, busy world filled with demands, expectations and activities. How might we experiment with ways to make space to focus on God? Some families have a time or place where technology is not permitted. Instead, they spend time talking with each other. Helping people practice time alone or with a good book is a gift to them in this world filled with distractions.

Learning from a story

As we look at this phrase "I'm listening," it appears that the opportunity for each person to truly listen to God can often depend on the mode of presentation. Although God can speak directly to the heart of an individual, I believe He expects us to be faithful in presenting His Word in ways that will connect with the listeners. For the pastor led to preach on a particular topic or a youth leader presenting God's Word, we need to put it in language that will be understood by those ready to listen – those who come hungry to hear and say to God, "I'm listening."

The pastor in this church made the invitation each week to come forward for prayer. A congregation member with autism spectrum disorder was listening to God's call. She was living in a place of unforgiveness towards Sue who worked in her group home several years ago. The problem, however, was that this was the 36th week that Lynnae had come forward for prayer. The pastor wondered how to handle this. I asked how he was praying with her. Lynnae told about the things Sue had done and then he asked permission to put his hand on her shoulder and they prayed together. At the end of the prayer Lynnae hugged the pastor and gave a big smile. The next week, however, Lynnae was back up front asking to forgive the same individual.

The pastor needed to know some more information about Lynnae. He needed to better work through getting to know the individual. Lynnae learns very little by ear, but she learns a lot through her eyes. I suggested the next time they write Sue's name on a sticky-note, carry it over to the cross in front of the church, and pray about forgiveness as taking that person and putting her with Jesus to take care of the problem. Lynnae didn't need to think about Sue anymore because Jesus would take care of the problem. I also suggested they leave the sticky-note there for the next week because coming forward for prayer was a habit. But when the pastor saw Lynnae, he could ask where they put Sue and see that she was forgiven and still with Jesus.

The next week Lynnae came forward and the pastor pointed out the sticky-note. She smiled and walked away. That was the last time she came forward for prayer about Sue. While they had talked about forgiveness 36 weeks in a row, Lynnae needed to understand it in a visual way. She was listening to God's call to come forward for prayer, but the pastor needed some different presentation tools.

Idea Bank for "I'm Listening" (Illumination)

1. Although each person with a disability is a unique individual, you will have a much greater impact if you involve more of the senses of those listening. That's actually true for each of us. For example, you could talk about the sword of the Spirit, but actually swinging a sword around as you talk will

increase the likelihood that people will connect with your words. By asking people to swing their arms as if holding a sword as you have them speak some phrases along with you will increase the possibility of hearing the information even more. If you are talking about being a prophet, priest, and king, consider having three hats with those words written on them. As you talk about each role or "hat" we wear as Christians, wear the acompanying hat. Providing hat patterns for people to make their own to wear as they review the points at home will really allow the concept to sink in more deeply. How can you add a prop, a set, an action, a drama, or a take-home piece that will reinforce the words you are speaking? Can't think of one? Share your lesson or message with someone who is a visual person in your group or congregation. Find a person who "thinks in pictures" and let them provide you with some ideas.

2. Think of the example provided in Scripture. When God said "Do this in remembrance of me," how did He set it up? God wanted us to remember what Jesus has done for us, and He made it totally possible for every type of learner to connect. The Lord's Supper is something that pulls in several sensory systems. We hear the words in Scripture, taste the wine and bread, smell the fragrance of the elements, touch them as we receive the elements, taste them, and often involve movement as we go forward or pass the elements to the next person. If we let Communion serve as our example, we will be all set! Think multi-sensory!

3. Boil down your lesson or message to one main point. What is the one big idea you want people to understand? As you pull in other points and sub-topics, remember to highlight your one big idea throughout the lesson. Perhaps you will have people repeat it with you. You might always display the "big idea" in PowerPoint or on a poster. You could save the posters to display to help people trigger the memory of your previous messages.

4. Some individuals might benefit from sitting with a mentor or interpreter. This person could quickly translate confusing phrases or answer questions as they arise. This person would be responsible for trying to have the individual connect with the message. It could be as simple as whispering "Jesus loves you, Matt" into the ear of the friend. The person might restate or clarify, "Pastor is talking about a flood, lots of water. Can you draw lots of water on this picture?" As the message continues, they would add elements to their picture story to reflect that Noah would be safe, just like Matt is safe with God. Training four people to be a mentor for one individual would allow each person to fit into that role one time per month. Those four people would get to know Matt and how he best learns and grows.

5. Add pictures. By using PowerPoint or other pictures, you will have a reference point for those who comprehend words more slowly or differently. Church school or small group leaders should have a bank of visuals to

draw from each week. If you can't find the pictures you want, use a digital camera to take some. Have friends dress up like characters or express a certain emotion on their faces.

6. Develop bulletins that can stand alongside the message. Have a person in your congregation who is savvy with a computer have the pastor's message a day or two in advance. Come up with activities that will go along with the message. If there is a verse you are highlighting, then do some type of fill in the blank activity with that verse. If you are talking about Mary and Joseph, have people draw in those characters beside the manger. What parts of the message could you turn into an activity sheet?

7. There may be times when a topic is very difficult for an individual with an intellectual disability. It's at those times when an alternate curriculum might be best. Including the individual in a portion of the worship service or age-appropriate class is excellent. The other portion, however, might be better spent with a mentor who can communicate in a more effective way. Remember, only do this for a PORTION of the time. By always moving an individual, the body of Christ is missing an important part. Preserve the body, and then provide portions of time for pullout instruction. Friendship Ministries has excellent materials one can use in these types of settings.It is a high quality curriculum focused on persons with intellectual disabilities.Materials are available through Faith Alive Christian Resources[1]. Bethesda Lutheran Communities[2] also has cur-riculum materials for persons with disabilities. Standard Publishing[3] has made all of their Church school and Vacation Bible School materials inclusive so that there are tips for connecting with children with and without areas of disability located in the materials prepared for the general group.

8. There are those individuals with disabilities for whom it appears there is very little understanding and connection with others. How does one allow this individual to listen? I believe that God wires each one of us to connect to Him in some way. Whether that method is by ear, eye, or touch, the wiring is there. As you include this person in your congregation, pray over that individual that God would speak directly to his or her heart and mind. Ask for God's Spirit to make a connection that humans appear to be unable to make. Praise God for His ability and knowledge to complete the wiring job.

9. Teach your congregation the sign for "I'm listening." Have them sign that throughout your message, as you get ready to repeat the "big idea" or another important concept.

10. You can make a telephone out of PVC pipe. Not only does it look like a telephone from a few years ago, it provides great feedback to the ear when you speak or whisper into it. Connect two corner pieces with a straight piece. Use the PVC pipe phones before your message. Let people

know there is a phone call from God. Have individuals say into that phone "I'm listening."

11. Know the individual. Get to know the gifts and needs of each person. An individual with a hearing loss may need an interpreter or a special sound system set up in the sanctuary. A person with low vision may benefit from larger print or books in Braille. PowerPoint without some type of verbal presentation won't connect with a person who is unable to see it. Do you need a ramp or special seating for a person with a physical difference? Get to know your people. Once you have done that, it might be helpful to establish a connection (done with confidentiality issues in mind) with others who know this person well. Find out what others have used to effectively interact with this person. Try a few new things. Be creative.

HELP (PETITION)

Hear me, Lord, and answer me, for I am poor and needy.
Guard my life, for I am faithful to you, save your servant who trusts in you.
You are my God; have mercy on me, Lord, for I call to you all day long.
Bring joy to your servant, Lord, for I put my trust in you.
Psalm 86:1-4

Children run to their parents or other people they trust when they are afraid. Often there are no words to express fear but it is quickly evident that the child is terrified. Sometimes the danger is real, sometimes it is perceived. Regardless of the cause, the child seeks protection and assurance.

Adults, too, experience fear. God tells us that we can come to Him for help. Perhaps we bring a desperate plea because of a life-altering experience. Perhaps we ask for help in making decisions or in relationships.

A congregation comes together in worship to ask for God's help. It may be for our own personal needs, for the needs of others, or for the needs of the world.

As parents we know the importance of our children trusting us enough that they can come to us when they are afraid. God invites His children of all ages and abilities to bring their fears and uncertainties to Him.

Why is it often hard to ask for help? Our culture teaches us that we should be self-sufficient. There is a perception that asking for help is a sign of weakness. In healthy human relationships and in our relationship with God, it is essential that we humble ourselves and acknowledge that we need others.

Learning from a story #1

It was obvious the man needed help. He had probably used that word many times each day of his life. This man was unable to walk. Daily care required others. He needed help moving, getting food, getting dressed, and making a living. His friends had heard about Jesus and wanted to take him to a place where they could witness a miracle. They knew that Jesus could make their friend walk. Carrying him on a mat, they found an obstacle. The crowd was too thick. The hope of getting this man to Jesus seemed slim in the large crowd. I'm not sure how long they brainstormed together before arriving at this idea, but they removed part of the roof and lowered the man in front of Jesus. Jesus healed the heart and body of this man because of the faith of his friends. What an amazing truth – the faith of a community of believers moved the healing hand of God. Not only do I see this as an example of the importance of holding up our friends with disabilities before God, I also see a group of people committed to modifications and accommodations. Use whatever word makes the most sense to you, but getting this man before Jesus required creative thinking and an alternate route.

Help. Sometimes we don't like to ask for that. It's much easier to be the helper than the helpee. Some of our friends with disabilities, however, are well acquainted with that word. While it might take me 30 minutes to get from my bed to the car, ready to face the workday, an individual who uses a wheelchair may find the morning routine taking much longer. While I can reach the top shelf at the local food store, an individual with a physical challenge may be unable to do that. "Help."

How easy it is for many of us to avoid that word "Help." After all, if I just work harder and longer, I can do it myself. That, however, is not the way God desires for us to live. Not only do we show pride by not acknowledging our daily need of God's help, He gives us a community where we are expected to ask for help. He expects us to support one another so that our areas of giftedness will complement another's area of need. Our needs, then, require the giftedness of others.

Learning from a story #2

It was such a difficult day. The drama team I directed was performing that morning, and I was exhausted. Life at school and home was more hectic than I could handle. Instead of asking for help, I just tried to up my performance and tried to put on a happy face in front of people.

I arrived at the church that morning and tried to use one of my smiles to cover up a sea of exhaustion. It was working. No one seemed to notice. Then Jonathan sat down beside me. I had been Jonathan's teacher when he was young, and now he played the role of Jesus in the play. Jonathan and I had known one another for 25 years. I, however, was typically in the teacher or leader role.

He reached his hand out for mine and said in halted and broken sentences (Jonathan has Down syndrome), "Mrs. B, you look sad today. I will pray for you." He did. Cover blown. And God used his words and presence in my life to heal my hectic and broken insides on that day.

On that day, Jonathan dug through the outer covering I had placed over myself in order to set me in front of God. He was the friend, I was the one on the mat desperately in need of the presence of Jesus Christ.

Don't ever assume you know which one is on the mat. As a church, we need to surround one another. What will it take to get each one of us before Jesus? What will it take to reach each individual? For some, it requires brainstorming and creative friends as are mentioned in the Bible. What changes need to be made in order for an individual to understand and enjoy a worship service? What additions or deletions need to be in place for someone to access the fellowship provided in a small group? Whether voiced or unvoiced, we need to ask for help from one another so that each one can stand face to face with God and make that same request to Him, "Help." Make a clear path for that conversation to happen.

Idea Bank for "Help" (Petition)

This will also include some educational changes you can make to help support the needs of some individuals in class-type settings.

1. As you use the word "Help" in your worship service, teach the sign language for this word.

2. Getting help from someone is certainly well within the understanding of individuals with disabilities. When you transfer that to asking God for help, it might make more sense to some individuals to have a picture of Jesus, an empty chair, or a specific place where people can bring requests for help. By writing out requests for help and placing them on that chair or by that picture, it allows you to also track God's answers. If someone is asking for help during a surgery, then it's powerful to go back to that written request for help and comment on God's answer. This is a great time to bring in the response of "thank you."

3. Although it's important to be ready to offer help to an individual, some people with unique gifts and needs have stories and issues that can seem overwhelming to us. Many times an individual will come to a person with a problem or situation and expect that individual to give an answer. It's important, however, to model for that person that you do not hold those hard answers – but you know who does. No matter what the situation, you know where to go with that hurt or feeling. You know that all of those issues are safe in God's hands. Teach individuals to go to God. It's great to talk to a friend, but God is the one who answers prayers. He is the hero – you are not. He is the source of all strength – you are not. Reroute the word "help" to the proper place – God.

4. In some small group settings, it's helpful to have pictures available during prayer time. A person with limited speaking ability may be able to point to a picture and ask for help using picture communication.

5. For some people, it's hard to access words when one is frustrated or anxious. Although a child or adult may use words to ask for help, some

people won't be able to ask verbally. It's important, therefore, to be mindful of having some type of non-verbal arrangement available for a child or adult who may need to leave a particular setting. For example, some leaders have a "break ticket" hanging on a wall. Instead of asking to be excused, an individual is welcome to grab that ticket and leave. It allows people with limited language (for either permanent or temporary reasons) a chance to make a request without using words. It's also a great system if the leader notices an individual is becoming stressed or anxious. The leader can take the ticket and hand it to the individual, suggesting that a break might be helpful.

6. There are certain individuals you know will need support and help to make church a happy and successful place. There are some other individuals who may benefit from some modifications, but they stem from learning needs, not physical needs. For example, a Church school class may have a child who receives support in school for reading and writing. When it's time to read aloud, that child may wish to crawl under the table. It's for these individuals for whom some simple changes may help increase happiness at church. Some individuals need accommodations in the area of reading. Here are some things you might be able to try:

Find the book or passage on a recording. The Bible in most versions is available for free on a Bible app called You Version.[1] Once downloaded on your device, it has a feature that will read the passage out loud.

Do partner reading where the individual is paired with a friend who can read the passage out loud.

Some individuals may need larger print.

Others may be able to participate by highlighting key words with a highlighter or highlighter tape.

Sometimes copying the book passage, enlarging the print, and using a different color background paper (like blue or green) can help an individual read the words more easily.

Some may be able to read pictures, and a friend could translate some of the passage by putting a small picture or icon by some of the words.

Sometimes it helps to practice in advance. If, for example, a class generally takes turns reading aloud, an individual might be assigned a section the week before so that he or she can practice that portion.

Find the same information at an easier reading level. If the story is from Genesis, one might be able to find a picture book or Bible story-book that shows pictures in addition to a more simplified text.

7. Writing is a complex task – even more difficult than reading. Some individuals need accommodations in the area of writing. Here are some things you might be able to try:

Use a partner. The pair must talk about what is written before it's put on paper, but only one person does the writing. Have two people, but only one final paper product.

Have an individual copy key words into blanks instead of trying to originate a whole sentence or paragraph. (Sometimes it's easier to copy from a paper beside the person than from a board or overhead.)

Lessen the amount of writing expected. Instead of a whole page, ask for a few key words.

Use technology. Have the individual put thoughts on a recording rather than on paper.

Supply a few options. Instead of writing, perhaps a picture or outline or collage might be appropriate.

Sometimes it's best to use a scribe. Have a leader or partner write for the individual.

Things like keyboards, larger sized pencils, and adapted crayons or markers can be very helpful. If appropriate, ask caregivers what tools would be the most helpful in the area of writing.

8. Many individuals need accommodations in fine motor activities and crafts. Here are some things you might be able to try:

Sometimes having a variety of sizes for scissors, markers, crayons, and other tools can be very helpful. Check teacher stores and catalogs for ideas.

Simple changes to a project can allow some people to participate. For example, instead of drawing animals on the paper, have the person put animal stickers on the paper. Instead of cutting out the objects and then gluing them down, have those objects pre-cut for the individual to glue.

If it's a project with multiple steps, sometimes it helps to explain the project and then sit beside the individual and do one yourself for the individual to follow.

Try to think through the steps of the project. What portions could the individual accomplish? You do the other parts.

Start thinking about the individuals in your class at least a day ahead. This will allow you to get ready and have the needed supplies available.

9. Have a team of friends do the thinking. It's helpful to have at least one other person to put together modifications. Just like the man in our Bible passage had faithful friends, sometimes it takes one person to move the tiles while another gets rope to lower the mat. Whatever the arrangements, multiple minds are almost always better than one.

10. Include input from the individual with the disability. Sometimes it's easy to ask for input from everyone else, but remember to talk to your friend about necessary accommodations. Is that chair comfortable? Which marker would you rather use? Would you like me to read this to you, or would you like a recording of the Bible passage? Include the preferences of the individual involved.

11. Be sensitive to those with milder needs. There are times when certain individuals prefer to have no accommodations, even when you know it might help that person. Some children, for example, would prefer to not be singled out when everyone else is using the same type of pencil. In this case, it might take some time to build trust with that person.

12. The Bible story about faithful friends is an excellent one to share in a Church school class or other child's group. Not only can you encourage the group to pray for a classmate and friend, it can also allow you to brainstorm with the group. How can we make it easier for Justin to be part of this class? What could we do during Bible story so he can answer a question? Children can be highly creative, and involving them in the discussion can also encourage them to be more involved with the friend.

13. As you involve peers, it's important to remember the difference between a "friend" and a "mother." In fact, you might want to spend some time role-playing the difference. I generally tell classes that Jason already has a mom. What Jason needs is a friend. Then I enjoy showing the difference between those two types of interactions.

14. As children and adults interact, be willing to give specific feedback. Instead of saying "I'm glad you are nice to Justin," try saying "I like the way you let Justin try his glue lid first, and then you asked if he wanted help. It's great to let him try it on his own, but you were right there to help out before he got frustrated." Not only are you giving a pat on the back, you are helping to shape future interactions. Whereas schools are building relationships that will last a few years, churches are building relationships that may last a lifetime. Justin and his friend may grow old together in this church community. You may be shaping this friendship for years to come.

15. Don't recreate the wheel when it comes to finding helpful modifications and accommodations. If allowed by parents, guardians, or the individual, check with the current school or placement to find out what has been

successful with an individual. Parents are a great source of information – ask them. In adult care homes, workers may be more than willing to share ideas with you. Don't be shy about asking.

Make sure to reference Appendix B. The Substitution Guide lists common activities we do in church settings with alternate options for that activity. Feel free to make copies from the website listed so that each church volunteer can reference this guide.

Are you hoping to equip your children and youth volunteers with some additional ideas for individuals who struggle with paying attention, sensory differences, reading, and writing? Consider the DVD called *Inclusion Tool Box: 52 Practical Ideas to Include Individuals with Disabilities*.[2] This 60 minute DVD is available at www.clcnetwork.org.

©Matt Hale

THANK YOU (GRATITUDE)

Praise our God, all people, let the sound of His praise be heard;
He has preserved our lives and kept our feet from slipping.
For you, God, tested us; you refined us like silver.
You brought us into prison and laid burdens on our backs.
You let people ride over our heads; we went through fire and water,
But you brought us to a place of abundance.
Praise be to God, who has not rejected my prayer
or withheld His love from me.
Psalm 66:8-12, 20

Learning to express thanks is one of the first emotions of relationship that many children learn. When someone gives something to them, does something for them, when love is expressed in any way, parents teach their children to respond with gratitude. It may be with words, a sparkle in the eye, a smile, some recognition that someone cares enough about them to express love.

In worship we have opportunity to express our thanks to God. Perhaps we name the reasons for our gratitude. Often it is easy to thank God for material blessings, but practicing the habit of naming and giving thanks for spiritual blessings can help deepen our gratitude to God. It also protects us from disappointment or discouragement when we pass through times when it seems our material blessings are limited. The focus on spiritual blessings can change our perspective from a sense of scarcity to abundance. Thanking God for all He has given us rather than grieving what we do not have leads to joy and contentment. Helping people identify God's many gifts – His faithfulness, patience, forgiveness – can help them express thanks, especially in difficult times.

Learning from a prayer

Please join me in this prayer of Thanksgiving for certain individuals through whom God has touched my life in profound ways. As I mention these individuals, perhaps you could begin your own prayer for similar people in your life.

Thank you, God, for Lana. She was an example to me of how you long to spend time with us. Lana would take any snippets of time I would give her. She loved to just hang out with me. Whether we had anything to say or not, she would just be with me. I know you love me that way too, God. I remember clearly the day that the newspaper reporter took several pictures of us together. She kept that article and memory with her all the time. Sometimes I think you hold me close to your heart like that too. I also know the day she got so jealous of my sharing attention with others, and she threw her shoe at me across the classroom. Thank you that I ducked in time. I'm sure you must get jealous too, God. I deserve to have a whole closet full of shoes whipped in my direction! Thank you for Lana and her love. Thank you for your love and grace. Thank you, too, that she is now with you – no longer hindered by lack of oxygen. Her face would turn purple, and now I think her face must glow from being in your presence. Thank you for Lana, the first friend of mine who happened to have Down syndrome.

Thank you, God, for John and Andrea. They both loved music so very much. They both had a zest and love for life. I enjoyed them as students and children of yours. For both of those children, they were with me one day and with you the next. You made me grow, God. You made me think about the importance of how I treated each child every day. You gave me a passion for making sure each one knew about you and made a commitment to you. I rejoice that now both children are released to praise you fully. Andrea's tongue, slowed by Down syndrome, and John's body, so easily thrown into seizures, are now completely unhindered as they praise you. I look forward to meeting them again, not as students, but totally as my sister and brother in Christ.

Thank you for Jessica. You taught me that spiritual warfare is real. You allowed me to witness the transformation that takes place when we accept Christ as Savior. I know that I had seen it before, but Jessica having autism spectrum disorder allowed me to see it with the social veil removed. I saw the instant transformation in her speech and countenance. I saw you enter her life, and she put up no barriers to block your entrance. I got to see the transformation from death to life in the face of a young girl. I hear your words through her. She has a profound relationship with you. "My body may have autism, but my spirit does not." Autism does not take away from her life with you. In fact, Jessica and you have something very special together. Actually, you and I have something very special together, too. Thanks for loving each one of us, searching us out, fighting for us, and being in relationship with us – a relationship that is unique to each one.

Thank you for Stu. When I asked for first grade volunteers to help support a child with Cerebral Palsy, he jumped in with all he had. He was so sad the day he got sick and had to stay home because he could not be with his friend. Stu, and so many others like him at my school, is a gift from you.

When I watch him delight in his buddy, it reminds me of the way you want me to delight in the people who surround my life.

Thank you for Lana, John, Andrea, Jessica, Stu, and so many more. You have enriched my life through them.

In the name of Jesus, Amen.

Idea Bank for "Thank You" (Gratitude)

1. Once again, teach the sign for "Thank You." You can use it in prayers, in songs, and in conversations with God and others.

2. Children learn at a very young age to say "Thank You." To allow that concept to transfer, practice on real people first. For example, you might like to give a friend a gift or treat and request that she sign or say, "Thank You." Then look at a picture of a flower or something else in nature. Tell your friend that God gave you that gift of a flower just like you gave her the gift of a candy treat. Together, you can say and sign "Thank You" to God.

3. Having a picture bank is an excellent way to talk about things for which we are thankful. Instead of trying to come up with an idea with no visual, it allows someone to get an idea or to point to a picture. I was in a worship service with an individual who has a picture board she uses for communication. As part of prayer requests, her mentor asked her to show what she was thankful for. After selecting an item, the mentor said, "Mary is thankful for Rob." That was incorporated into the prayer that day.

4. Psalm 136 is an excellent one to use in a responsive reading. By teaching the phrase (perhaps even in sign) "His love endures forever," one can participate in the worship service by reading a portion of Scripture. Repetition is often very helpful for individuals with an intellectual disability. Depending on your type of service, sometimes it's helpful to use more repetitive phrases. For example, by having everyone say, "Thanks be to God" each time you have finished reading Scripture, it will allow participation each week for certain individuals.

5. Focus on the glass being half full. Let's face it, there are many people who struggle each day with difficult circumstances. Although it's easy to be consumed with those issues, it's also important to allow that individual to focus on the gifts that God has given. Begin a routine of starting a conversation by saying "Today I am thankful for ____." If you do that each time you see a particular individual, he will begin to prepare for your conversation and focus on those gifts. It's also a great conversation starter at a family meal time.

6. We generally think about a cornucopia being a Thanksgiving decoration. Consider having one that is available year round. Use a basket as a cornu-

copia and turn the top of the basket into a piggy bank slot. As people share a story or event, you can quickly grab a pen and write out, "Deb is thankful for her new job." Put it in that display. Every once in awhile, take the slips out and thank God for those items that people have submitted.

7. Ask an artist in your church to make you some pictures, or look for other pictures that show attributes of God. For example, God is strong. God is a healer. God loves. As you show the picture, the group can pray along, "Thank you, God, for being strong. Thank you, God for being a doctor healer." Having the pictures to go along with the words can help make prayer more concrete.

8. Has your congregation or family been blessed by the presence of an individual with a disability? Perhaps you would consider thanking God for that individual. What gifts has God given your group because of the presence of that person? As an image-bearer of God, what do you see in that person that makes you think about God?

If you want to delight in some other stories of the gifts that persons with disabilities bring to our communities, considering reading *Body Building: Devotions to Celebrate Inclusive Community*[1] written by Barbara J. Newman. It's available at www.clcnetwork.org

WHAT CAN I DO? (SERVICE)

What shall I return to the Lord for all His goodness to me?
I will sacrifice a thank offering to you and call on the name of the Lord.
I will fulfill my vows to the Lord in the presence of all His people,
In the courts of the house of the Lord - in your midst, Jerusalem.
Praise the Lord!
Psalm 116:12, 17-19

In a loving relationship we want to put our emotions into action and offer something to the one we love. Parents teach children that a response to love is to do something helpful and loving in return. A child may willingly help with work around the house when parents explain the significance of returning love through actions.

In our relationship with God, His love for us leads us to serve Him and the people He puts into our lives. A valuable conversation with others can help them explore what they can do to express love for others. They may wish to do something special for a person who they love at home or church or school. Help them be creative.

Learning from a story

At the beginning of this book I referenced green and pink puzzle pieces, with the color green representing our strengths and the color pink our weaknesses. When we say to God, "What can I do?," we are offering up our green (and even our pink) areas in His service. That is just as true for a person who is typically developing as it is for a person who has a disability. Service is an expectation for each one of us.

At our annual Harvest Festival, the community was treated to candy at each event. One of our candy passers held the bowl on her lap as the rest of her body was immobilized due to Cerebral Palsy. Each child got a smile from her and a piece of candy. She was using a gift she had to serve others, and everyone was blessed by it!

Idea Bank for "What Can I Do?" (Service)

1. Remember, the place to begin is getting to know the individual. If you skipped over part 3 of this book, please go back to complete those activities. Remember, not everyone with a disability is gifted to be a greeter. Discover the individual's gifts and needs.

2. Plug that person in to your community based on the strengths and gifts. Although each individual is unique, here are a few ideas:
   greeting
   coffee serving
   library assistant
   stuffing member mailboxes
   picking up attendance sheets
   support person with children
   intercessor – praying for the needs of others
   creator of artwork
   building maintenance
   yardwork
   office support person
   counting the offering, sorting the money
   taking attendance
   making food
   host for small group
   visiting senior citizens
   any match of gift to a situation at church

3. It might be helpful to have a mentor with an individual to serve as a coach for awhile. By greeting with another individual, you can form a bond with a peer as well as learn skills from one another. Although there might be a time when an individual can make coffee on her own, having a mentor to teach and guide initially is important.

4. Look for ways to include that individual in existing service projects at your church. For example, if your youth group is going on a mission trip, do you have a youth group member with a disability that might also be able to go along? Perhaps part of the service opportunity would be to form a circle of support around this individual so that he or she could participate in the project. If you have a weekly food distribution or food pantry, perhaps an individual could work in this area.

5. Once again, you may want to teach the sign language for "What can I do?"

6. If you have a digital camera available, you might want to take pictures of a variety of people in your group, including an individual with a disability. As you ask for people to make a commitment, "What can I do?," you might want to have those pictures cycling through on a screen. "Here are some

people from our church. God wants you to serve Him. What can you do?" By including that individual, you not only speak to the individual, but also to your entire community.

7. Sometimes an individual with unique gifts and needs can be an opportunity for service for others in your church. Forming support groups around an individual can provide mutual blessings. In the school setting we often offer children a circle of friends. This group agrees to befriend the individual and support the needs as well as celebrate the gifts. CLC Network has put together a program called G.L.U.E. teams in churches. G.L.U.E. stands for Giving, Loving, Understanding, and Encouraging. Taking the circle of friends concept, church volunteers agree to surround an individual or family. They get to know one another and commit to supporting that person. If your church has interest in creating a G.L.U.E. team, make sure you get a copy of the manual and training DVD.[1] It's available at www.clcnetwork.org

BLESS YOU (BLESSING)

O my soul, bless God.
From head to toe, I'll bless His holy name!
O my soul, bless God, don't forget a single blessing!
He forgives your sins – every one.
He heals your diseases – every one.
He redeems you from hell – saves your life!
He crowns you with love and mercy – a paradise crown.
He wraps you in goodness – beauty eternal.
He renews your youth – you're always young in His presence.
God has set His throne in heaven; He rules over us all. He's the King!
So bless God, you angels, ready and able to fly at His bidding,
quick to hear and do what He says.
Bless God, all you armies of angels, alert to respond to whatever He wills.
Bless God, all creatures wherever you are –
everything and everyone made by God.
And you, O my soul, bless God!
Psalm 103:1-5, 19-22 (The Message)

When we practice the Vertical Habits we are reminded of the blessings God has given to us, we bless God out of gratitude to Him and we extend that blessing to other people. Perhaps blessing is the most difficult concept to teach to young children. Maturity is needed to understand God's blessings to us and the ways we can bless others.

But even the youngest among us can experience the assurance and comfort of a blessing. Some parents speak a blessing to their children when they put them to bed. Families may express a blessing when they gather around the table for a meal. We can speak a blessing over one another in the body of Christ.

A worship service typically ends with a blessing. God's blessing is given to His people and they are charged to go out to be a blessing to others. In some churches people are encouraged to open their hands to receive the blessing. For many people this can be especially meaningful to experience God's blessing for them.

Learning from a story

Every day of the year, my mom would set out breakfast and serve us with love and respect. Generally by about the end of April, however, I began to search mom's Ladies Home Journal magazine. Anticipating Mother's Day in May, I would hunt for those amazing ideas the family could do to "bless" mom. I read what other families had done, and it sounded pretty good. Mom would like breakfast in bed. Mom would enjoy having a whole day without touching the dishes. That craft on page 42 looks really cute. She would not expect to have a large gift, but when the actions of her family back up the words they say ("I love you, Mom"), it blesses her. Actions plus words really say it all.

"Bless you" is not only something we can say to God, but I believe we need to back up those words with actions. 2 Corinthians 1: 3-4 says, *Praise be to the God and Father of our Lord Jesus Christ, the Father of compassion and the God of all comfort, who comforts us in all our troubles, so that we can comfort those in any trouble with the comfort we ourselves have received from God.* This passage (other translations use the word "Bless" instead of "Praise") certainly lets us know that as we bless God as the one who gives us comfort, we in turn are expected to actively pass on that comfort to others. Another passage in James says, *What good is it, my brothers, if a man claims to have faith but has no deeds? Can such faith save him? Suppose a brother or sister is without clothes and daily food. If one of you says to him, 'Go, I wish you well; keep warm and well fed', but does nothing about his physical needs, what good is it?* James 2: 14-16 As we reach our hands out to God and say "Bless you," I would imagine God is a bit like Mom on Mother's Day. She is blessed by the actions that back up those words.

What if the passage from James were worded a bit differently? "What good is it, brothers and sisters in Christ, if a person raises their arms to God and cries out 'Bless you!' but there are no actions to back up those words? Suppose there is a brother in your church community who has Down syndrome. That person is not allowed in Sunday school or the worship service. If one of you says to him, 'We are the body of Christ. You were made in God's image, and you have an honored place here as part of that body', but you do nothing to create that spot, what good are your words?"

1 Corinthians 12 is not a suggestion; it's a picture and command of how God expects us to live with others in the body of Christ. As you take steps to back up those words with your actions, I know you will have created a concrete way to bless God. God's heart is open and bleeding for those He sent us – those whom many have turned away. A church is to be His agent of healing in this world, and many persons with disabilities will testify to the hurt and pain they have experienced from exclusion. Exclusion does NOT bless God. Inclusion, and our obedience to His heart, will bless God.

Say it and do it! Then watch God's blessing fall on your community in ways you cannot yet imagine.

Idea Bank for "Bless You" (Blessing)

1. Get your congregation ready for words and actions. It's always best to start with Scripture. God is very clear with what He expects of us. Perhaps your group needs to hear very clearly what God is saying in His Word. Challenge them to begin to put actions with those words. Find a coordinator – someone who is willing to focus attention on supporting the gifts and needs of those who have a disability in your community. Perhaps that coordinator will need the support of a committee. Have those people get to know the individuals and put together individual plans for each person. The format I recommend for this process is spelled out in the *G.L.U.E. Training Manual.*[1]

2. Don't allow persons with disabilities in your community to be content, either, with just saying the words to God. Allow each person opportunities to put actions to words. Include individuals in ways to praise God. Include all members in service projects and postures of prayer. Give opportunities to speak and act – even if the speaking and acting comes in unique packages.

3. Get the word out in your community. Is your church ready to put action behind the words "Everyone Welcome"? If so, your community is aching to hear those words. I can guarantee you that there are families at home during your worship time because a family member has not been welcome in the place they know as "church." Get ready for God to grow your church community. There is a mission field out there ripe for God's touch through you.

4. As you teach people the meaning of "Bless You," you may want to teach the sign for those words. You may also want to use the example many individuals have witnessed in a church setting. As the pastor delivers God's blessing to the people, often a pastor will raise his or her arms over the group. As you say "Bless You" to God, have people raise arms to God.

5. Appoint people within your congregation to create visuals to go along with the phrases in the Psalms where the writer blesses God. These can be used as part of a responsive reading or a "blessing" display with references.

6. Have individuals think about who God is. You may want to use picture cards to cue these thoughts, or have people write down a sentence or two on paper. "God, you are holy." "God, you are strong." "God, you are enormous." Whatever people know to be true about God, have them speak it out. Give people a chance to bless God by telling Him who He is.

7. Many of the suggestions written in the section "Love You" might be helpful here as you use music and songs to say "Bless You" to God.

Make sure you reference Appendix C. It contains many activities that churches have done with Vertical Habits. The ones we have included are easy to adapt and use with an inclusive congregation. Also note that while we have focused the efforts of this book on including persons with disabilities, our congregations often include persons who may be new believers, people from a variety of backgrounds and cultures, and persons from a variety of age groups. Many congregations have found Vertical Habits to be a way to welcome each one into the conversation with God. May God show you many ways to use this concept within your congregation.

COMMENTS FROM SCHOOLS AND CHURCHES THAT LEARNED AND PRACTICED VERTICAL HABITS

From fifth graders:

...I worship the one true Father in heaven, the maker of heaven and earth, the one who made me the way that I am – not strong in math, but strong in art. He made me that way for a reason, for a plan that only He knows... I worship because it brings me closer to God, like if you hang out with a friend and get to know them more. Soon enough they could be your BFF. God can be like that too. Just talk to Him and He will be your BFF one day.

...What I learned about worship and God, is that it does not matter where I am or what I am doing. I can always worship God. I don't only have to worship Him in church or at chapel. For example, I might be in the computer lab taking a MAP test that seems boring. If I try my best, I am doing it for God's glory because He gave me the brain that I have.

...Whenever I think of how big God is and how much He loves us, I think of my cousin Noah stretching his arms out as far as they can go while he is saying, "so big!" God is so much bigger than that!

...For "I'm sorry," each class received bags of sand, symbolizing sin. Students carried them as they participated in normal activities. Classes talked about how sin weighs them down and inhibits their lives. In a Friday praise time, the teacher explained how confession means laying down our sins. Then the students placed their 'burden bags' at the cross.

Vertical Habits gave students a worship language that spilled over into academics. During a reading lesson, one student commented, "The girl in that story is not practicing the Vertical Habit of forgiveness."

In a Christian high school setting where the students and teachers come together each day for worship, during the year of Vertical Habits, one month was devoted to lament. "That was an incredible month of personal testimonies, of crying out to God in chapel. It really came across to students that it's okay to wonder, to question why. God is big enough to handle our frustrations, our anger, whatever is going on in our life."

"Psalms for Families"[1] by Robert and Laura Keeley use the Psalms to encourage faith formation in children and youth. They've discovered that when all ages interact with the Psalms, they nurture a common language for life together with God. They've learned how to create access points into the Psalms for preschoolers on up. "We included psalms of lament to make sure children get to experience that we can come to God with our sorrows," Laura Keeley says.

When children engage with the Psalms, they become aware that God hears them, and learn language they can use when they feel like singing a praise chorus or when their world has been shattered. The Psalms demonstrate how to tell God we're sorry or ask God for help.

A young college student was given the responsibility of making sure everyone got on the bus. She assigned every choir member a phrase from Psalm 24. She'd get on the bus and say, 'The earth is the Lord's and everything in it.' The next student would say, 'The world and all who live in it' and so on. They would recite the entire Psalm each time they got on the bus. And they knew if anyone was missing, because they knew the Psalm and who said what line. Psalm 24 became an important part of that choir tour, and they ended up reciting it in their concerts.

Adults can help children see that whenever the people in Psalm 107 were hungry, thirsty or in chains, they cried out to God. God responded, and they gave thanks. Youth can color-code the Psalm's repeated pattern of 'trouble – God's response – our thanks.' They can talk about how God acts in our daily lives and how we thank Him.

Tom Long, director/writer of the Christian drama group Friends of the Groom, worked with five metro Cincinnati churches on Vertical Habits.[2] He reports that congregations approached the same habits differently, depending on their theological traditions and congregational makeup.

Focusing on what we do in worship helps remove attention from preferences of style. One church reported that for two years they had been in the midst of considerable congregational discord, which contributed to a loss of many young families. There was a critical need to rebuild trust between various factions within the church, as well as a need to renew worship in a manner that reached out to children, youth, and their parents. This church reported, "Vertical Habits is bringing a fresh element to worship by focusing on the purpose behind worship, rather than engaging in a debate about the style of worship. It has helped us emphasize the elements of worship that draw us together as one body."

The concepts of Vertical Habits may at first appear simplistic. Yet the churches who have taken time to learn and teach these concepts have found them both challenging and profound. Marc Nelesen, who pastored the congregation at Third Christian Reformed Church in Zeeland, Michigan, noted, "In a day where true, intimate communication is breaking down, even these simple, pithy words become incredibly complex and difficult. The Word that became flesh should be easier than all these other words that we have."

Another congregation reported, "We have learned so much from our children, who have contributed drawings and devotional entries on the various Vertical Habits. I am truly amazed at the simultaneous profundity and simplicity of their understanding of these habits as they relate to God. Their very honest and very real responses to the Vertical Habits have really challenged many of us to approach God with a 'child-like' heart. We learned to appreciate those with disabilities because one of our concentrations was the hand signs of each of the Vertical Habits. The children especially got involved in this."

One church created stations that allowed people to learn about and experience Vertical Habits through hands-on activities. One group expressed "I'm Sorry" by laying a road down on the floor complete with forks in the road where you had to make a decision about which way to turn. Sometimes in life we make good decisions but we also make bad ones for which we have to repent. When we repent, God washes us clean. This group symbolized that forgiveness by putting a car wash over the road (PVC pipe with blue streamers) and had people remember that God washes them clean as they walked through the car wash. Another station had a locked treasure chest with a key that did not work. A person trying to unlock the chest needed to ask for help, something that was surprisingly challenging for many people.

A church of inner city youth called their project the *Relationship Toolbox*. They found it provided the tools for young people to interact with each other and with God.

In a clinical, residential setting with young people, Vertical Habits proved to be a simple way to build relationships and give expression to emotions these young people had not been able to express.

For more information including reports, videos, and free resources see http://worship.calvin.edu/resources/resource-library/showcase-vertical-habits-worship-and-our-faith-vocabulary/

Why? by Kyle Ragsdale

VERTICAL HABITS IN A HORIZONTAL COMMUNITY

ANY GOOD PLAN HAS TWO PARTS

So often in planning for an inclusive setting, the focus is on creating a plan for the individual with the disability. This is very important, and hopefully your tool box is bursting with the practical ideas contained in this book. It's important to remember, however, that your plan is only half done. All good plans have two parts – one for the individual and one for the "others."

There are many church stories where planners and organizers have extensive plans for the individuals that equal the planning done within a public school. These plans, however, can often amount to very little when they have not considered how the plan interweaves with others in the environment.

My favorite story happened during a worship service. There was a new family starting to attend a church. One of their family members was quite outgoing and would shake hands and introduce herself to others. She enjoyed music and also being at the new church. She also lives with autism spectrum disorder. One Sunday, the pastor was in the middle of his sermon. In a loud voice, his words and the attention of the entire congregation were interrupted with "STOP! NO! DON'T!" Everyone was startled and looked around for the source of the emergency. Without missing a beat and a smile on his face, the pastor said, "I was looking forward to a chance to introduce you to my new friend Claire. Her parents gave me permission to tell you (this is important – you can't give out information without permission) that Claire enjoys coming to church here. Many of you have already shaken her hand. She does have sensitive ears, however. She happens to have autism spectrum disorder and probably she heard a sound that bothered her ears. No worries. Today I will count her as my cheering section." And he went on with his message.

About five minutes later, Claire called out the exact same words in the exact same volume. How many people do you suspect turned around that time? Zero. They had the information they needed to include Claire on that day. The pastor not only made sure there was a place for Claire, he also focused on the second part of the plan – he provided information to the congregation so they could best receive Claire and the gifts she brings to their community.

Whether it's information, training, specific teaching, a sermon series, a newsletter article, or a short video,[1] what will others need in order to best receive the gifts that individual brings to your community? I have written several books and prepared recorded trainings. Of these tools, about half are to support the individual, and the other half supports information for peers, leaders, and volunteers in the environment. Working in an inclusive Christian school setting since 1989, I have learned the value of making sure there is a plan for everyone involved.

PLAN FOR THE PEERS

Whether children, youth, or adults, consider how you will resource your congregation, school, or small group. In many respects, there are two levels of preparation. On one hand, you may want to begin a general preparation without bringing in the gifts and needs of a specific individual. Consider the following:

1. Have the governing board of your church or organization study the biblical reasons for including persons with disabilities. A great place to begin is Appendix A in the *G.L.U.E. Training Manual*.[2] It's intended to be shared and studied for this purpose.

2. Look into your church denominational materials. Many have statements and even extensive resources that support the topic of including persons with disabilities. Some denominations even have support personnel who can give ideas to your community.

3. Consider highlighting this topic as part of a sermon series. If you need ideas, there is great support at www.crcna.org/disability.

4. As a church community or small group, consider a book study on a topic related to including persons with disabilities. *Body Building: Devotions to Celebrate Inclusive Community*[3] is one example of a resource that could be used with multiple ages.

5. Show a video that highlights this topic. While there are many available, finding one from a Christian perspective is helpful. It will anchor people in the reasons why we include from a biblical perspective. Check out www.clcnetwork.org for some possibilities.

6. Invite a local speaker, parent, or individual with a disability to come to your community and give a presentation.

7. Make a puzzle piece display that highlights the gifts and needs of each member of your group. Instructions are available in the *Inclusion Awareness Kit*[4] available from www.clcnetwork.org.

8. Stock your library or resource center with books and materials dedicated to this topic.

9. An additional resource you can use with children is *Your Feet, My Shoes*[5] by Sarah Bolt. It's available at www.clcnetwork.org.

While general information and information from a Scriptural perspective are important, it's also important at times to equip peers to receive a specific individual. In order to illustrate this, let me tell you about day 1 of every school year at Zeeland Christian School. It's my busiest day. Flying from room to room, with permission from parents, I do a very specific talk in each classroom that includes a child with a disability. I tell them about the child's "puzzle piece" – the greens and pinks of that person. We celebrate what that person can do well. Sometimes the child will demonstrate areas of gifting for the group. I also give information at their level of understanding about the child's story. We talk about Down syndrome as I build a tower with colorful blocks and reference the number of chromosomes. We talk about how that makes some things easier and some things more difficult. As a group, we brainstorm ways to come around this individual and get commitments from friends to be part of a network of support. Then I send a letter home with the students so that the parents of peers will also better understand the stories their child will tell at the dinner table throughout the year. It also opens doors for playovers and birthday party invitations.

Why is day 1 so important at both school and church? I want to be the first one in line to hand out eyeglasses. I want the peers to be able to interpret the actions and words of this classmate from an accurate and positive perspective. Peers WILL form an opinion and perspective, but it's almost always better if they can use my eyeglasses to view this peer.

I had a conversation with a parent the other day. She was hesitant for me to talk to the peers. It was day 35 of school and I was waiting for the parent's blessing. Mom said to me, "But I don't want my child to be singled out and have some label attached to my child." While I totally understand this and can do a talk without using words like autism spectrum disorder or AD/HD, I mentioned to this mom that the children had already attached a label to her child. It was the label called "bad kid" or "weird." If we do nothing, that label will stick; if I can distribute a new way of looking at her son – one that highlights his God-given gifts and needs, one that impresses upon the peers that EVERYONE has areas of gifts and needs, then her child may be free to better enter into peer relationships.

This process has become so important in inclusive settings that it was the topic of the first book I wrote. If you don't have it on your shelf, I suggest you get a copy of the second edition of *Helping Kids Include Kids with Disabilities*.[6] This will give you the vision-casting lesson plans you can use with children and youth. For adults, I suggest using the resources found in the *G.L.U.E. Training Manual*. If you are a representative of a school, I recommend the books *Nuts and Bolts of Inclusive Education*[7] and *Circle of Friends Training Manual*.[8] Many resources can be found at www.clcnetwork.org to help support you in this effort.

PLAN FOR THE LEADERS AND VOLUNTEERS

While it's important to resource the peers, don't forget your leaders and volunteers. Here are some possible ways you can resource them:

1. A helpful process and tool is explained in the *G.L.U.E. Training Manual*. It's called a Welcome Page and it takes information collected from parents and individuals and turns it into a one-page description of a specific individual. Your leaders will need this information.

2. Sponsor one training a year on this topic. We recorded four 60-minute training DVDs on different topics. Try those or you could invite a local speaker to your community. If you have a high number of individuals with autism spectrum disorder, then train your leaders and volunteers in this topic. If you have struggling readers and writers, consider a training in this area. Are you struggling with behavior management issues? Equip your leaders.

3. Give brainstorming opportunities. Gather together all the volunteers who surround John. Talk about what is working well and what areas are still hotspots. Brainstorm together some possible solutions.

4. Gather up resources. Whether written or recorded, develop a shelf of helpful materials.

Let us help you. CLC Network is committed to resourcing your community. Perhaps you would like to sponsor an event in your area. Combine with other local churches and invite us to equip your leaders. Some denominations even will give grants to help make this happen. Do you have questions about one specific individual? Through an actual visit or review of video footage, we will consult with your church community and give ideas for you to try. We have materials and expertise. Don't recreate the wheel.

FINAL PRAYER
FOR THE READERS

Romans 15:13

May the God of hope fill you with all joy and peace...

What a beautiful picture. God doesn't do things in small measures. He doesn't want to give you a drip or two of joy and peace; He wants to FILL you with these things.

May the God of hope fill you with all joy and peace as you trust in Him...

How important that as we get to know individuals, set up environments where we can introduce a family member or friend to Jesus Christ, or seek to build inclusive worship settings we place our trust in God. He is the one who knit together that individual. He is the one who gives the gift of salvation. He is the one with the command to function together as one body. So, please don't trust in Barbara J. Newman or Betty Grit. We hope and pray we've been used by God to be helpful to you, but look to God for His wisdom, direction, and strength.

May the God of hope fill you with all joy and peace as you trust in Him, so that you may overflow with hope...

What a job we get to do! We get to pour God's hope over the people He places in our lives. One of the reasons He fills us is so that we overflow His hope on others. There may be some very hope-starved people in your life. People who don't see the God-given gifts in themselves or others. People who thought they would never have a church home. People who heard the voice of the church say "We don't have anything for you here" and they mistook that for the voice of God. May God use your words and actions to pour out something different. May they experience godly words and actions that bring hope and healing into their lives. Go ahead – pour it out.

May the God of hope fill you with all joy and peace as you trust in Him, so that you may overflow with hope by the power of the Holy Spirit.

Isn't it excellent that we don't have to wake up each morning and try to do these things on our own strength? The perspective and power comes from the Holy Spirit. May He invade your life and your imagination. May He give you pictures and glimpses of what He sees and pass that on to you. May your own life be one of movement in Christian Formation. May you be in constant conversation – not just on the Sabbath – but speaking those words in conversation with God throughout all of your day. "I Love You." "Thank You." May the habits of these words become so natural, your conversation with God becomes like breathing. And as you use the materials in this book, may God bless each conversation with His presence and guidance.

Be filled with His joy and peace.

Trust Him.

Pour His hope on others.

Be filled with the Holy Spirit.

May the God of hope fill you with all joy and peace as you trust in Him, so that you may overflow with hope by the power of the Holy Spirit.

Amen.

I'm Listening by Kyle Ragsdale

NOTES & REFERENCES

Scripture quoted from the *New International Version* unless otherwise noted.

Introduction

1. Dallas Willard wrote and presented on spirituality. Three well-known publications of his are: *Renovation of the Heart*, published in May 2002; *The Divine Conspiracy*, released in 1998; and his most recent book, *Knowing Christ Today*, released in 2012. For more information see www.dallaswillard.org.

2. N .T. Wright is a leading New Testament scholar, and retired Bishop of the Anglican church. Some of his works include:
   - *Following Jesus: Biblical Reflections on Discipleship*, Wm. B. Eerdmans, 1997.
   - *Surprised by Hope: Rethinking Heaven, the Resurrection, and the Mission of the Church*. SPCK, HarperOne, 2008.
   - *The Case for the Psalms: Why They Are Essential*. HarperOne, 2013.
   - *Simply Good News: Why the Gospel Is News and What Makes It Good*. HarperOne, 2015. (release date 6/15/2015).

3. Quote was posted on www.ZCS.org during 2013-2014 school year.

Planting Our Feet on Common Ground: The Puzzle Piece Perspective

1. Mark Stephenson, head of Disability Concerns for the Christian Reformed Church, has said this in conversation, and includes this idea in much of his writing and work, as can be seen at www.crcna.org/disability.

2. The *Inclusion Awareness Kit* is a packet of lesson plans and materials to teach the idea of puzzle pieces, produced by CLC Network, available at www.clcnetwork.org/clc-store.

Most Important Place to Begin: Getting to Know the Individual

1. Voicemails can be converted to written text using a service from Verizon for $2.99/month (as of October, 2014); information at: www.verizonwireless.com/wcms/consumer/products/visual-voicemail.html or for AT&T provider phones, see www.att.com/esupport/article.jsp?sid=KB412330#fbid=HPLEvuo5eVy for information about such services.

Accessible Gospel

1. These videos offered a way to share the Gospel message:
   - *Finding Nemo*, Walt Disney Pictures with Pixar Animation, 2003.
   - *Beauty & The Beast*, Walt Disney Pictures, 1991.
   - *Star Wars Episode IV A New Hope*, 20th Century Fox with LucasFilm Ltd., 1977.

2. *Adventures in Odyssey* is a radio show and cartoon (video) broadcast on Christian stations, and has been sold, packaged in episodes for purchase, or to listen online. Find out more at www.whitsend.org.

3. YouVersion is a free App available for download to many electronic devices such as phones, iPads, Nook readers, which offers the full text of the Bible, as well as a way to access sermon notes if the church uses this service (also free to upload sermon notes). See www.YouVersion.com for information and to download the adult App. For Kids, see www.bible.com/kids to download this picture Bible with animation and other great tools.

4. Eric Carle first published *The Very Hungry Caterpillar* (Penguin Putnam) in 1969. Since then it has been published many more times, and made into videos, used as flash cards, toys, lesson plans, crafts and many other educational activities.

5. Barbara J. Newman, *The Easter Book*, Faith Alive Christian Resources, 2003. Available at www.clcnetwork.org/clc-store and www.Friendship.org.

Inclusive Worship

1. http://network.crcna.org/disability-concerns/ask-your-youth-group-do-accessibility-audit is a great place to start on assessing your church's accessibility.

Love You

1. Barbara J. Newman, *The Easter Book* (see above)

2. Barbara J. Newman, *Autism and Your Church: Nurturing the Spiritual Growth of People with Autism Spectrum Disorders*, Faith Alive Christian Resources, 2011 (Revised & Updated from 2006). Available at www.clcnetwork.org/clc-store and www.Friendship.org.

I'm Sorry

1. Barbara J. Newman, *Helping Kids Include Kids with Disabilities*, Faith Alive Christian Resources, 2012 (Revised from 2001). Available at www.clcnetwork.org/clc-store.

2. Sarah Bolt, *Your Feet, My Shoes*, CLC Network, 2009. Available at www.clcnetwork.org/clc-store.

3. The *Inclusion Awareness Kit* (see page 83)

4. Barbara J. Newman, *Body Building: Devotions to Celebrate Inclusive Community*, CLC Network, 2011 (Revised from 2009). Available at www.clcnetwork.org/clc-store.

Why

1. Neil Anderson, *The Bondage Breaker: Overcoming Negative Thoughts, Irrational Feelings, Habitual Sins*, Harvest House Publishers, 2006 (first published 1990).

I'm Listening

1. From Faith Alive Christian Resources, Friendship Curriculum includes 3 Bible Study Series on *God Our Father*, *Jesus Our Saviour*, and *Holy Spirit Our Helper*, as well as other studies and resources. Find them at www.Friendship.org.

2. Bethesda Lutheran resources include kits and full lessons on Lutheran catechism topics, prayer models and many other areas. Their selection of materials for adults with intellectual disabilities is quite large. See http://store.shopbethesda.org/storefront.aspx.

3. Standard Publishing's HeartShaper® Children's Curriculum provides teachers with extra helps for adapting classroom activities to include children with different abilities. Beginning in Fall 2015, the special-needs icon found throughout the teacher guides identifies activities that are especially appropriate for including kids with different abilities. Additional tips, encouragements, and ideas for adapting activities can be found on each age-level's *Resources* CD (included in the teacher convenience kits) and on the HeartShaper website, www.heartshaper.com.

Help

1. YouVersion (see page 83)

2. This training presentation by Barbara J. Newman was recorded and is available in a one hour DVD, *Inclusion Tool Box: 52 Practical Ideas to Include Individuals with Disabilities* DVD, CLC Network, 2011. Available at www.clcnetwork.org/clc-store.

Thank You

1. *Body Building* (see page 84)

What Can I Do

1. Barbara J. Newman and Kimberly Luurtsema created the *G .L.U.E. Training Manual: Working Closely with Congregations to Help Them Better Understand, Support and Include Each Other* (CLC Network, 2009). The accompanying Training DVD (*Making Room: Cultivating Communities of Inclusion – G.L.U.E. Training DVD*, CLC Network, 2012) helps those desiring to implement G.L.U.E. understand how to use the Manual. Both are available at www.clcnetwork.org/clc-store.

Bless You

1. *G.L.U.E. Training Manual* (see above)

Comments

1. Robert J. and Laura Keeley, Psalms for Families, found online (printable) at http://worship.calvin.edu/resources/resource-library/psalms-for-families-devotions-for-all-ages-introduction.

2. Tom Long, director, playwright, and chief storyteller for Friends of the Groom Drama Group out of Cincinnati, Ohio. Information at www.friendsofthegroom.org.

Vertical Habits in Horizontal Community

1. Videos, reports, and free resources compiled by Betty Grit can be found at: http://worship.calvin.edu/resources/resource-library/showcase-vertical-habits-worship-and-our-faith-vocabulary.

2. *G.L.U.E. Training Manual* (see above)

3. *Body Building* (see page 84)

4. *Inclusion Awareness Kit* (see page 83)

5. *Your Feet, My Shoes* (see page 84)

6. *Helping Kids Include Kids with Disabilities* (see page 84)

7. A history of Inclusive Education as well as a guidebook with printable forms to execute an inclusive education program in a Christian school setting, Barbara J. Newman wrote *Nuts and Bolts of Inclusive Education* (CLC Network, 2013). Available at www.clcnetwork.org/clc-store.

8. Barbara J. Newman, *Circle of Friends Manual*, CLC Network, 2009. Available at www.clcnetwork.org/clc-store.

APPENDIX A

What is green for this individual? What does this person enjoy doing? What strengths do you see? List 3-5 words or phrases.

What is pink for this individual? What do you see as struggles or areas of need? List 2-3 words or phrases.

"GETTING TO KNOW ME" SHEET

What CAN the individual do?

How does the individual take information in?

How does the individual get information out?

What movements can the person do?

Does the individual have any sensory sensitivities?

What equipment, safety measures, or supports might be important for this person?

Who needs to know this information?

To download a PDF of Appendix A, go to clcnetwork.org/accessiblegospelappendices

APPENDIX B

SUBSTITUTION GUIDE

Each individual in your group is a God-designed mixture of strengths and challenges. In any given activity, you will have some people who flourish and others who flounder. Make sure you think through the activities you are doing and make the needed modifications and substitutions so that each person can participate in a meaningful way.

Activities the individual finds challenging	Substitutions you can make
Cutting	Use a spring-loaded scissors or small-sized scissors Give the person a set of pre-cut items Give the person a set of pictures with only minimal cutting left to do on each item Outline with thick marker the lines and curves that need to be cut
Writing	Use a pencil or pen the individual finds successful (larger, weighted, triangular, mechanical, broken, and small) Turn the writing surface into a 45 degree angle Put a pencil grip on the pencil or pen Work in pairs by having both people write their names on the paper to signify ownership. Ask one to do the writing but they must talk about the answer together before it gets written. Make a copy and send it home with each partner Assign a "secretary" to do the writing Downsize; assign the individual to write the answer to number 1 while the others write the answers to numbers 2-5
Coloring	Use different size crayons Outline in marker the object(s) you want the person to color Have the individual "hop on your hand" as you color together Have a page pre-colored except for a couple of items Assign a buddy to play "Simon Says" where the person tells the buddy what item to color and which color to use
Speaking	Give a choice to write or speak the answer Have a set of pictures or objects available and ask the person to point to the picture or item Ask questions that require a head nod or shake or give a thumbs up or thumbs down response Ask for a response that requires a movement for an answer

Activities the individual finds challenging	Substitutions you can make
Listening	Provide as many visuals as possible Add signs and gestures to your presentation Give directions only one at a time Ask the individual to repeat the directions one at a time Have a finished model to follow Use an amplifying system to highlight the voice of the speaker
Looking	Describe with words the items you are showing or holding up Produce the visuals on high contrast paper (black on yellow) Enlarge the visuals Find items the individual can touch or hold
Moving	Depending on the movement that is a challenge, discover the body part that works well and make a substitution (e.g., instead of running to the area, point to the area; instead of pointing, look at the item) Assign a pair where the individual completes one portion while the buddy completes the challenging movement Alter the activity for all in the group so that movement is eliminated or changed to something all can do together
Reading	Read to the individual Record what needs to be read and play the recording Assign a buddy and have one person be the reader and one person be the listener and picture watcher Prepare and have the individual practice the reading passage ahead of time Color code or color highlight what should be read

Be creative. This is a list to get your brain thinking about substitutions so you can find one or discover one that will work for each person in your group.

To download a PDF of Appendix B, go to clcnetwork.org/accessiblegospelappendices

APPENDIX C

VERTICAL HABITS RESOURCES

Appendix C provides you with a sampling of the resources available on the Vertical Habits website. While I have applied this topic to including persons with disabilities, the original project was not focused on persons with disabilities. Vertical Habits is something each member of your congregation, as well as visitors, could grow and learn from.

Make sure you visit the website to discover many additional resources you can use and adapt for your own worship setting:

http://worship.calvin.edu/resources/resource-library/showcase-vertical-habits-worship-and-our-faith-vocabulary/

RESOURCE 1

A t-shirt logo designed by Kris Moore, Chaplain at Cincinnati Children's Hospital, Cincinnati OH.

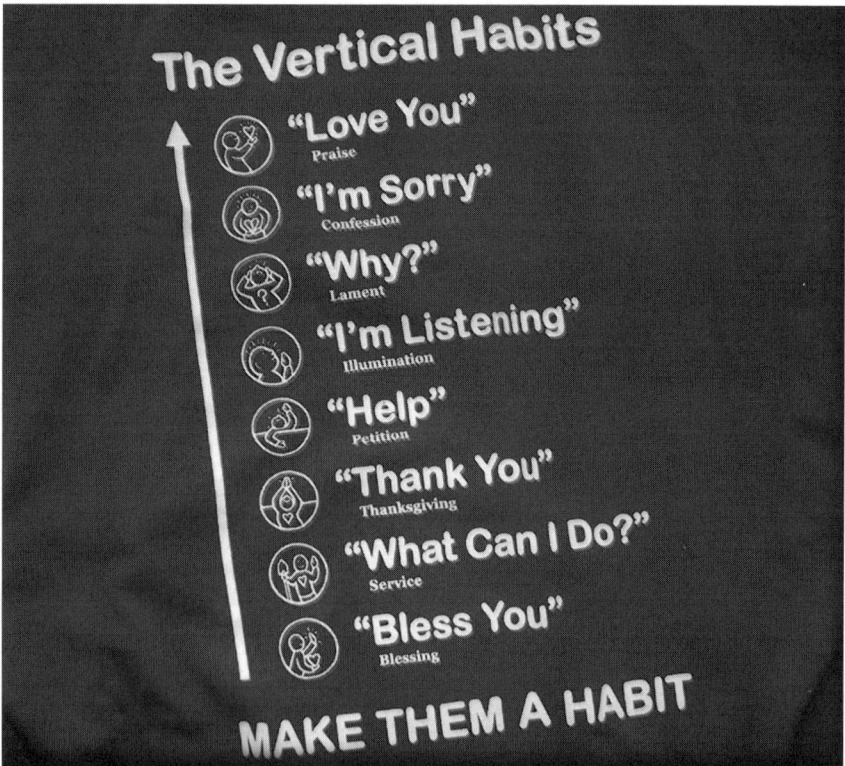

The Vertical Habits

"Love You" Praise

"I'm Sorry" Confession

"Why?" Lament

"I'm Listening" Illumination

"Help" Petition

"Thank You" Thanksgiving

"What Can I Do?" Service

"Bless You" Blessing

MAKE THEM A HABIT

RESOURCE 2

The next 33 pages are a set of devotions prepared for First Christian Reformed Church in Pella, IA.

"Love You"

"I'm Sorry"

"Why"

Our Psalm Adventure

"I'm Listening"

with

"Help"

the Vertical Habits

"Thank You"

"What Can I Do"

"Bless You"

This program is made possible through a Worship Renewal Grant from the Calvin Institute of Christian Worship, Grand Rapids, MI with funds provided by the Lilly Endowment Inc.

First Christian Reformed Church - Corner of West Second and Liberty, P.O. Box 321, Pella, Iowa 50219
641-628-2321, firstcrc@iowatelecom.net

"LOVE YOU" – PRAISE

Love is the foundation of any close relationship. Expressions of adoration or affection are the lifeblood of friendships, families, and our relationship with God. There's a lot more to worship than praise, but praise is the basis for worship.*

Choose one of the following Psalms of Praise/"Love You" to read each day this week; then pick one of the suggested activities to do per day.

Recommended "Love You" Psalms: 47, 95, 100, 146, 150

Optional "Love You" Psalms: 1, 3, 5, 8 19, 20, 21, 25, 26, 28, 29, 42, 47, 48, 53, 57, 65, 66, 67, 72, 75, 84, 87, 92, 93, 95, 96, 97, 98, 100, 103, 104, 105, 107, 108, 111, 113, 114, 115, 116, 117, 118, 128, 132, 138, 145, 146, 147, 148, 149, 150*

1. Think of words or phrases that praise God and begin with these letters:

L _____

O _____

V _____

E _____

Y _____

O _____

U _____

*Faith Alive Christian Resources – *Psalms for All Seasons*

2. **"Love You" Lord, for you are:**

1. _____
   _____
   _____

2. _____
   _____
   _____

3. _____
   _____
   _____

3. **We love God for who He is.** Choose one verse from today's Psalm – draw or sketch a picture of it.

4. Write a Haiku poem. Haiku poetry has 3 lines. Lines 1 and 3 have 5 syllables and line 2 has 7 syllables. This is an example:

Sing Praises to God
Salvation belongs to you
Bow down and worship

_____

_____

_____

5. Create a word cloud of the Psalm: Go to www.wordle.net and type in 10-12 words from the Psalm, or just interlock them below. For example:

```
          J
SALVATION
H        Y
O
U
THANKSGIVING
```

6. Write a verse or phrase from this Psalm that you will use in your prayer today or design a Prezi – Go to www.prezi.com to create an artistic PowerPoint style presentation using words from the Psalm.

7. **Praise – "Love You"**

   1. What does this habit mean to you?

   2. How do you use this habit when you are with other people?

   3. How do you use this habit when you talk to God?

   4. What do think about this habit? Can you use it in prayer?

"I'M SORRY" – CONFESSION

Confession is about honesty, and honesty is essential to a relationship. Hiding things destroys trust; "coming clean" allows a relationship to flourish. This is why we confess our sin in worship.*

Choose one of the following Psalms of Confession/"I'm Sorry" to read each day this week; then pick one of the suggested activities to do per day.

Recommended "I'm Sorry" Psalms: 25, 32, 51, 78, 130

Optional "I'm Sorry" Psalms: 25, 27, 32, 38, 42, 51, 66, 78, 79, 86, 90, 102, 104, 123, 130, 139, 143*

1. **Think of words or phrases that express sorrow for sin to God and begin with these letters:**

I _____

M _____

S _____

O _____

R _____

R _____

Y _____

*Faith Alive Christian Resources – *Psalms for All Seasons*

2. "I'm Sorry" Lord, because:

1. _____
   _____
   _____

2. _____
   _____
   _____

3. _____
   _____
   _____

3. We are sorry before God for who He is and what we've done. Choose one verse from today's Psalm – draw or sketch a picture of it.

4. **Write a Haiku poem. Haiku poetry has 3 lines. Lines 1 and 3 have 5 syllables and line 2 has 7 syllables. This is an example:**

Forgive all my sins
Save me from my wickedness
Restore joy to me

_____

_____

_____

5. **Create a word cloud of the Psalm: Go to www.wordle.net and type in 10-12 words from the Psalm, or just interlock them below. For example:**

```
          J
SALVATION
H        Y
O
U
THANKSGIVING
```

6. Write a verse or phrase from this Psalm that you will use in your prayer today or design a Prezi – Go to www.prezi.com to create an artistic PowerPoint style presentation using words from the Psalm.

7. Confession – "I'm Sorry"

1. What does this habit mean to you?

2. How do you use this habit when you are with other people?

3. How do you use this habit when you talk to God?

4. What do think about this habit? Can you use it in prayer?

"WHY" – LAMENT

Lament is also a matter of honesty. The psalmists model for us unflinching expressions of sadness and anger toward God as part of a close relationship with God. It's not disrespect; it's a way of placing all our emotions and experiences before the one we want to hear them the most. Following this model, our worship, too, must give a biblical voice to the sadness and anger worshipers bring in their hearts to worship.*

Choose one of the following Psalms of Lament/"Why" to read each day this week; then pick one of the suggested activities to do per day.

Recommended "Why" Psalms: 13, 22, 61, 80, 126

Optional "Why" Psalms: 3, 5, 7, 9, 10, 12, 13, 17, 22, 26, 28, 31, 39, 41, 44, 58, 59, 61, 69, 71, 74, 79, 80, 83, 85, 88, 94, 109, 123, 126, 137, 141*

1. **Think of words or phrases that give voice to your lament before God and begin with these letters:**

   W _____

   H _____

   Y _____

*Faith Alive Christian Resources – *Psalms for All Seasons*

2. **"Why" Lord? I am sad or angry because:**

1. _____

_____

_____

2. _____

_____

_____

3. _____

_____

_____

3. **We lament before God because we are sad or angry.** Choose one verse from today's Psalm – draw or sketch a picture of it.

4. Write a Haiku poem. Haiku poetry has 3 lines. Lines 1 and 3 have 5 syllables and line 2 has 7 syllables. This is an example:

Why, O my God, why
Death, disease, and disaster
Heal our brokenness

_____

_____

_____

5. Create a word cloud of the Psalm: Go to www.wordle.net and type in 10-12 words from the Psalm, or just interlock them below. For example:

```
          J
SALVATION
H        Y
O
U
THANKSGIVING
```

6. Write a verse or phrase from this Psalm that you will use in your prayer today or design a Prezi – Go to www.prezi.com to create an artistic PowerPoint style presentation using words from the Psalm.

7. **Lament – "Why"**

   1. What does this habit mean to you?

   2. How do you lament when you are with other people?

   3. How and when do you lament when you talk to God?

   4. Some say that lamenting should not be part of the happy Christian life. What do you think about lamenting? How important is it to lament in the Christian life?

"I'M LISTENING" – ILLUMINATION

Without listening, there is no real dialogue. Listening opens the way for a relationship to happen. Before we go to God in worship, we say that we will listen to God's words.*

Choose one of the following Psalms of Illumination/"I'm Listening" to read each day this week; then pick one of the suggested activities to do per day.

Recommended "I'm Listening" Psalms: 19, 25, 85, 119:1-16, 119:89-112

Optional "I'm Listening" Psalms: 19, 25, 27, 36, 43, 85, 95, 119:1-16, 119:89-112*

1. **Think of words or phrases that indicate you are listening to God and begin with these letters:**

L _____

I _____

S _____

T _____

E _____

N _____

I _____

N _____

G _____

*Faith Alive Christian Resources – *Psalms for All Seasons*

2. **"I'm Listening" Lord, because you are:**

   1. _____
      _____
      _____

   2. _____
      _____
      _____

   3. _____
      _____
      _____

3. **We listen when God speaks.** Choose one verse from today's Psalm where God speaks, or we listen – draw or sketch a picture of it.

4. Write a Haiku poem. Haiku poetry has 3 lines. Lines 1 and 3 have 5 syllables and line 2 has 7 syllables. This is an example:

Speak to me, O Lord
God whose Word created all
Give me ears to hear

_____

_____

_____

5. Create a word cloud of the Psalm: Go to www.wordle.net and type in 10-12 words from the Psalm, or just interlock them below. For example:

```
          J
SALVATION
H         Y
O
U
THANKSGIVING
```

6. Write a verse or phrase from this Psalm that you will use in your prayer today or design a Prezi – Go to www.prezi.com to create an artistic PowerPoint style presentation using words from the Psalm.

7. Illumination – "I'm Listening"

1. What does this habit mean to you?

2. How does listening to God influence your daily activities and conversations with others?

3. How do you listen when you talk to God?

4. What do think about listening? Can you use "listening" while praying?

"HELP" - PETITION

When we're in trouble, we turn first to the ones we trust the most for help. And so we ask God in worship to provide for our needs and deliver us from evil.*

Choose one of the following Psalms of Petition/"Help" to read each day this week; then pick one of the suggested activities to do per day.

Recommended "Help" Psalms: 46, 54, 86, 91, 121

Optional "Help" Psalms: 3, 9, 13, 14, 18, 22, 23, 27, 31, 39, 43, 46, 51, 54, 56, 61, 63, 70, 80, 86, 91, 97, 102, 121, 124, 125, 130, 136, 137, 142, 143, 146*

1. **Think of words or phrases used to ask for help and begin with these letters:**

    H _____

    E _____

    L _____

    P _____

*Faith Alive Christian Resources – *Psalms for All Seasons*

2. **"Help"** me Lord, because you are:

1. _____

   _____

   _____

2. _____

   _____

   _____

3. _____

   _____

   _____

3. **"Help"** me Lord. Choose one verse from today's Psalm where God hears a cry for help – draw or sketch a picture of it.

4. Write a Haiku poem. Haiku poetry has 3 lines. Lines 1 and 3 have 5 syllables and line 2 has 7 syllables. This is an example:

Speak to me, O Lord
God whose Word created all
Give me ears to hear

_____

_____

_____

5. Create a word cloud of the Psalm: Go to www.wordle.net and type in 10-12 words from the Psalm, or just interlock them below. For example:

```
            J
SALVATION
H         Y
O
U
THANKSGIVING
```

6. Write a verse or phrase from this Psalm that you will use in your prayer today or design a Prezi – Go to www.prezi.com to create an artistic PowerPoint style presentation using words from the Psalm.

7. **Petition – "Help"**

   1. What does this habit mean to you?

   2. What makes it hard to ask for help from others? From God?

   3. How do you use this habit when you talk to God?

   4. What do you think about helping? Can you ask God to help without being able to act?

"THANK YOU" - GRATITUDE

"Thank You" is the counterpart of "Help!" The two stay in balance, placing our cries for help in the context of gratitude for help and goodness in the history of a relationship. In worship we offer our thanks to God for all God has done for us.*

Choose one of the following Psalms of Gratitude/"Thank You" to read each day this week; then pick one of the suggested activities to do per day.

Recommended "Thank You" Psalms: 30, 65, 66, 100, 136

Optional "Thank You" Psalms: 9, 18, 30, 34, 40, 65, 66, 67, 70, 75, 92, 97, 100, 107, 116, 122, 123, 124, 131, 136, 138, 144, 146*

1. Think of words or phrases that express thanksgiving and begin with these letters:

T _____

H _____

A _____

N _____

K _____

Y _____

O _____

U _____

*Faith Alive Christian Resources – *Psalms for All Seasons*

2. "Thank You" Lord, because you...

1. _____

_____

_____

2. _____

_____

_____

3. _____

_____

_____

3. We say "Thank You" to God. Choose one verse from today's Psalm that speaks of thanks to God – draw or sketch a picture of it.

4. Write a Haiku poem. Haiku poetry has 3 lines. Lines 1 and 3 have 5 syllables and line 2 has 7 syllables. This is an example:

Tell of God's wonders
My heart overflows with thanks
You are very great

_____

_____

_____

5. Create a word cloud of the Psalm: Go to www.wordle.net and type in 10-12 words from the Psalm, or just interlock them below. For example:

```
            J
SALVATION
H       Y
O
U
THANKSGIVING
```

6. Write a verse or phrase from this Psalm that you will use in your prayer today or design a Prezi – Go to www.prezi.com to create an artistic PowerPoint style presentation using words from the Psalm.

7. Gratitude – "Thank You"

   1. What does this habit mean to you?

   2. How do you use this habit when you are with other people?

   3. How does your life express gratitude to God?

   4. Write or pray a prayer filled with gratitude.

"WHAT CAN I DO" – SERVICE

If we take a relationship seriously, we want to turn our words into actions, to offer to do something in service. In worship, we go out with commitment to serve in the kingdom of God.*

Choose one of the following Psalms of Service/"What Can I Do" to read each day this week; then pick one of the suggested activities to do per day.

Recommended "What Can I Do" Psalms: 1, 86, 112, 116, 132

Optional "What Can I Do" Psalms: 1, 22, 26, 37, 40, 46, 47, 48, 50, 51, 54, 66, 67, 72, 86, 87, 96, 97, 98, 100, 101, 112, 116, 117, 132, 138*

1. Describe ways to serve God or neighbor that begin with these letters:

S _____

E _____

R _____

V _____

I _____

C _____

E _____

*Faith Alive Christian Resources – *Psalms for All Seasons*

2. Lord, "What Can I Do?" Use me to:

1. _____
   _____
   _____

2. _____
   _____
   _____

3. _____
   _____
   _____

3. **When we are committed to God, we want to serve Him and others.**
   Choose one verse from today's Psalm where God speaks and we respond
   with service – draw or sketch a picture of it.

4. Write a Haiku poem. Haiku poetry has 3 lines. Lines 1 and 3 have 5 syllables and line 2 has 7 syllables. This is an example:

God, what can I do
Use me Lord, use even me
Fill me with your love

_____

_____

_____

5. Create a word cloud of the Psalm: Go to www.wordle.net and type in 10-12 words from the Psalm, or just interlock them below. For example:

```
          J
SALVATION
H       Y
O
U
THANKSGIVING
```

6. Write a verse or phrase from this Psalm that you will use in your prayer today or design a Prezi – Go to www.prezi.com to create an artistic PowerPoint style presentation using words from the Psalm.

7. Service – "What Can I Do?"

1. What does this habit mean to you?

2. How do you serve other people?

3. How does your service express your gratitude to God?

4. How do you listen for God's answer to "What Can I Do?"

"BLESS YOU" – BLESSING

When we part ways with someone, we wish them health and peace until we reunite. In worship, we leave by blessing God's name and hearing God's blessing for us.*

Choose one of the following Psalms of Blessing/"Bless You" to read each day this week; then pick one of the suggested activities to do per day.

Recommended "Blessing" Psalms: 1, 67, 84, 112, 128

Optional "Blessing" Psalms: 1, 3, 14, 20, 23, 24, 32, 33, 37, 39, 52, 67, 69, 72, 84, 103, 106, 107, 112, 115, 121, 123, 125, 128, 133, 134*

1. **Think of words or phrases that name blessings God has given you and begin with these letters:**

B _____

L _____

E _____

S _____

S _____

I _____

N _____

G _____

*Faith Alive Christian Resources – *Psalms for All Seasons*

2. "Blessings" we receive from God or share with others:

1. _____

   _____

   _____

2. _____

   _____

   _____

3. _____

   _____

   _____

3. **"Blessing"**. Choose one blessing from today's Psalm – draw or sketch a picture of it.

4. Write a Haiku poem. Haiku poetry has 3 lines. Lines 1 and 3 have 5 syllables and line 2 has 7 syllables. This is an example:

Wrapped up in blessings
Like a fuzzy warm blanket
Perfect contentment

_____

_____

_____

5. Create a word cloud of the Psalm: Go to www.wordle.net and type in 10-12 words from the Psalm, or just interlock them below. For example:

```
          J
SALVATION
H         Y
O
U
THANKSGIVING
```

6. Write a verse or phrase from this Psalm that you will use in your prayer today or design a Prezi – Go to www.prezi.com to create an artistic PowerPoint style presentation using words from the Psalm.

7. Blessing – "Bless You"

   1. What does this habit mean to you?

   2. How do you use this habit when you are with other people?

   3. How do you number your blessings when you talk to God?

   4. God blesses you to be a blessing. How might you bless someone today?

To download a PDF of Appendix C, resource 2, go to clcnetwork.org/accessiblegospelappendices

RESOURCE 3

A collage of the many pieces of visual art created around the theme of Vertical Habits.

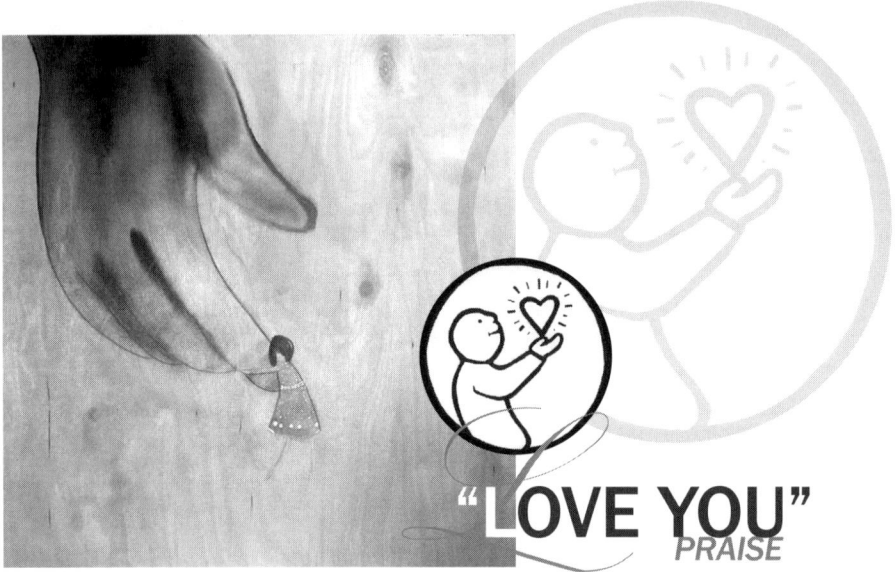

"LOVE YOU"
PRAISE

Love You by Kyle Ragsdale

"I'M SORRY"
CONFESSION

I'm Sorry by Kyle Ragsdale

With thanks to Dawn Rotman at Grand Haven Christian School.

VERTICAL HABITS

ADORATION ("I LOVE YOU LORD!")

We love God for who He is!
Choose a name or description of God from the list and draw a picture of it.

Comfort of the sad	Creator of all
Eternal source of knowledge	The first and the last
Fountain of wisdom	Giver of life and health
God of all power	God of all times and places
God of earthquake, wind, and fire	God of holy love
God our helper	Great ruler of the world
Healer of the sick	Light of the world
Only one	Our teacher
Our refuge and our strength	Redeemer and deliverer
Rock of all creation	Searcher of our hearts
Shining glory	Strong God of truth

INTERCESSION ("HELP LORD!")

**We often pray to God when we need help with something.
Asking others to keep us in their prayers regarding certain needs
is another way to strengthen us.**

Ask someone what they would like you to pray for in regard
to a need they may have.

Share a need of your own that you would like that person to pray for.

Each of you should write that need on a prayer card, which you can keep
somewhere important, so you will remember to pray for each other.

LAMENTATION ("WHY LORD?")

We have so many questions for God!
Because our God is so BIG, He could never provide us
with all the answers that we seek.
We just aren't capable of understanding everything He does!

Share with each other 1 or 2 questions that you want to ask God.

THANKSGIVING ("THANK YOU LORD")

God has given us so much for which we should be thankful!

Working together, draw a small line while mentioning something
that you are thankful for.

See how many lines you can draw!

DEDICATION/SERVICE
("HERE I AM, WHAT CAN I DO NOW LORD?")

As Christians, we are to be God's hands.
We need to seek out ways that we can show God's love through our actions.

"Cook up" a plan with someone to do something special or helpful for
someone you both know.

If possible, keep it a secret so as to give God all the glory!

CONFESSION ("I'M SORRY LORD")

When we sin, we need to bring it before God and say we're sorry.
If we do this, He is faithful and will forgive us of that sin –
erasing it completely, making us pure.

Create an image with Play-Doh that represents a sin
that you have committed.

When it is finished, smash it into a blob and put it away –
representing forgiveness.

PROCLAMATION ("I'M LISTENING LORD")

God speaks to us through His Word.

Ask someone to tell you their favorite passage out of the Bible.

Ask them how God "speaks to them" through this passage.

BENEDICTION ("BLESS YOU")

Bene-diction means "good say" in Latin.
We can "pray" good things on someone by saying a blessing to them.

Practice saying this blessing in Swahili together:

Bwana *(bwah-nah)*   **awabariki** *(ah-wah-bah-ree-kee)*
Mi *(me)*   **le** *(leh)*   **le** *(leh)*

(In English: May God give you a blessing evermore)

To download a PDF of Appendix C, resource 4, go to clcnetwork.org/accessiblegospelappendices

You can color in this bookmark as you complete each Vertical Habit.

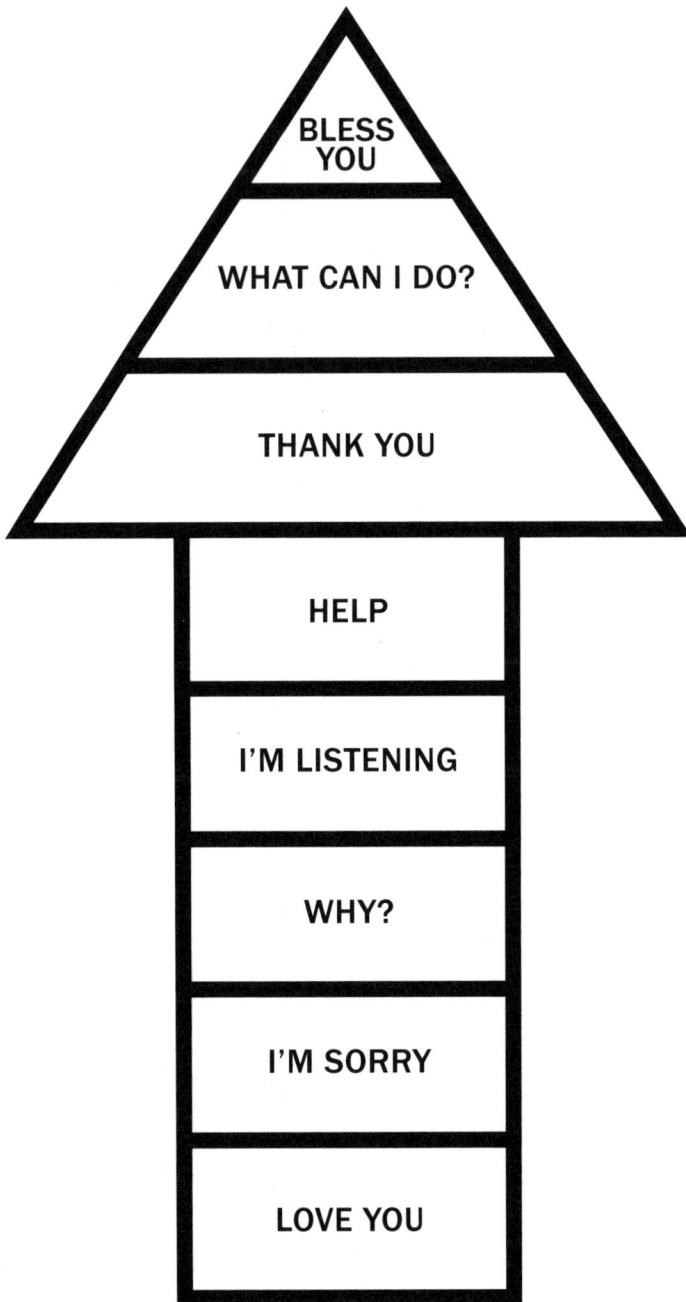

BLESS YOU

WHAT CAN I DO?

THANK YOU

HELP

I'M LISTENING

WHY?

I'M SORRY

LOVE YOU

GO VERTICAL!

ABOUT THE AUTHOR

Barbara J. Newman is a church and school consultant for CLC Network. She is the author of several books and is a frequent national speaker at educational conferences and churches. In addition to writing and speaking, Barb enjoys working in her classroom at Zeeland Christian School.

ABOUT THE AUTHOR

Barbara J. Newman is a church and school consultant for CLC Network. She is the author of several books and is a frequent national speaker at educational conferences and churches. In addition to writing and speaking, Barb enjoys working in her classroom at Zeeland Christian School.